HI-TECH
JOBS
FOR
LO-TECH
PEOPLE

HI-TECH
JOBS
FOR
LO-TECH
PEOPLE

William A. Schaffer

American Management Association

New York • Atlanta • Boston • Chicago • Kansas City • San Francisco • Washington D. C.
Brussels • Mexico City • Tokyo • Toronto

Library of Congress Cataloging-in-Publication Data

Schaffer, William A.
    Hi-tech jobs for lo-tech people / William A. Schaffer.
      p. cm.
    Half title: Hi-tech jobs for lo-tech people.
    Includes bibliographical references and index.
    ISBN 0-8144-7867-0
    1. High-technology industries—Vocational guidance—United States.
I. Title.   II. Title: Hi-tech jobs for lo-tech people.
HF5382.5.U5S288   1994
620'.0023'73—dc20   94-15767
                                                      CIP

Printing number

10 9 8 7 6 5 4 3 2 1

Contents

Acknowledgments

I wish to thank all the people who have contributed to this book. First and foremost, my gratitude to the more than seventy people, all "lo-tech," whom I interviewed, and whose interest in the project sustained me over the months. Your observations are the heart of the book.

Walt and Linda Brown's enthusiasm, good humor, and deep knowledge of many aspects of the high-tech industry were essential to the conception of the work and to its execution; they are the busiest people I know of in the industry, yet they made themselves available freely.

Barbara Graves was the first person who said to me, "That's a good idea," and for that alone I'm very thankful. Her critique of my proposal was my first experience with a professional editor; I survived it fairly well. Her knowledge of literary midwifery also got the proposal before my agent, Bill Gladstone of Waterside Productions, Inc. Without Bill's faith and backing, the project would have been stillborn.

My editor at AMACOM, Andrea Pedolsky, patiently annotated the first version I submitted to her. Her annotations were preceded by a "B−," which at first I took to be my grade. It was only after I still got B minuses after rewriting that I realized she was merely abbreviating my name. Working with her was a pleasure.

Very special thanks to my copy editor, Alice Manning, to whom I am deeply indebted for her painstaking work on the manuscript.

Scott McNealy is the president and CEO of Sun Microsystems, and therefore my ultimate boss. Thanks, Scooter, not only for being a superb leader (ahem!), but also for your comments on how nontechnical people get involved with and succeed in this industry.

Bob Daubenmire is a friend and management development consultant whose deep understanding of what makes organizations tick contributed in valuable ways to answering that perennial high-tech question: What in heck is going on here?

Amy Moore and Sri Rajeev, friends and colleagues at Sun, valiantly read and critiqued several chapters. There is nothing lo-tech about these two!

Thanks, too, to Ray Hendess, who responded like a hero to my midnight call about a certain hard disk whose contents appeared to be beyond recovery. I owe you, buddy!

My son Paul provided the artwork, as well as many a bemused chuckle.

Finally, my lovely and patient wife, Gesine, carefully and thoughtfully read every word of the manuscript, spotting inconsistencies, confusing statements, and lots of other problems with the text. I think I got most of them!

Introduction

This book exists because I spilled a glass of wine on my neighbor—or, rather, on her new Gucci pocketbook. She looked fresh out of college, and she had the seat next to me on a flight from Washington to San Francisco. The bag was new and must have had wine-repellent properties, because there was no obvious permanent damage. Of course I apologized profusely. This led to conversation, and, this still being North America, albeit at 40,000 feet, I asked her the standard question: "What do you do for a living?"

"I've got my degree in art history," she said, naming a well-known eastern college. "But since there weren't any jobs in my field, I started out substitute teaching for a couple of years. Then I got a job as a receptionist, and that's what I've done for the last eighteen months or so."

We talked some more. It was obvious that she was intelligent, well educated, and articulate. "Do you have any long-term plans?" I asked. "You don't intend to work as a receptionist forever, do you?"

"I hope not," she laughed. "I'm not really sure. Back in junior year I knew I couldn't get a job if I stayed in my field, but I loved it so! Right now I'm trying to save some money so I can get over to Europe this summer with my friends!"

"Did you ever consider working in a high-tech field?" I asked. "The computer industry, for example."

"Are you kidding?" she said, her eyes widening. "I don't know anything about computers—no one would want me. I'm interested in something creative, and technology sounds so boring!" She smiled again. "I guess those are three pretty good reasons."

I let it go. Nevertheless, that little exchange stuck with me, and caused me to raise the subject with a friend who is a senior manager in a Fortune 200 company. I asked him what skills he considers fundamental to success in the high-tech industry. My friend is an engineer and very technical, so I was surprised at his reply:

Excellence in communication. That means listening, writing, speaking, all aspects of communication. Listening is especially sensitive, because that implies a lot of social skills. Being able to determine what a person is really saying beyond the words themselves. Understanding what is driving him. Communicating outward also is important. What is the effect going to be on others if I say something this way or that way? Will it, for example, be seen as a challenge? What words do I choose?

After all, that is what 95 percent of your people really do all day long. In many companies, in order to get to the higher-paying jobs, people have to get into helping others do their jobs better. Working through others by managing, coaching, planning. All the things you would get out of a classic education.

Later I put my friend's remarks alongside the conversation I'd had with my co-passenger. The two didn't compute, as we say in the industry. She had given three reasons for not considering a high-tech job. First, she didn't know anything about computers. But so what? How much did you really have to know about computers, at least to get in the front door? Couldn't you at least get started, then learn what you needed to know after you got a job? Or get some kind of short-term training and use that to leverage yourself in? "They wouldn't want me," she thought. Well, perhaps art history wasn't much in demand, but this young woman would be because she was smart and articulate. Would there be room for her creativity? Absolutely! The industry is changing so fast that there are no rules; most positions are loosely defined, expanding and twisting into new shapes like polymorphs. Yes, there is plenty of room for creativity. Also, high-tech jobs pay well enough so that she could have art history as an avocation, and actually fly around to visit the Pitti Palace, the Louvre, even the graves of Sian.

I found myself wishing I could talk once again to my History of Art companion; I wanted to explain why looking into high-tech jobs makes excellent sense. First, many high-tech positions require no technical knowledge at the entry level, and sometimes even at fairly high levels. Second, the industry needs well-educated, creative people to fill these nontechnical positions, because without them the technology can't get out of the labs. Third, the high-tech industry is fast-moving, exciting, and fun. What would have been her reaction to my three points, I wondered. I supposed that she might well have had a "show-me" attitude. And then she might have said, "Even assuming that everything you say is true, what on earth am I supposed to do about it in practical terms? And even if I got a job, what would it be like in such a place for someone like me? It would be totally different. Who will help me get started?"

Pretty good questions. And as I thought more and more about it, I thought of more and more questions, more than I had the answers to, and probably more than could be covered in a flight between Washington and San Francisco. So I decided to write this book.

This book is about career choices. It is written for people who have been working for a while, and who want to make a change. Some of you will have been in the workforce for a few years, others for much longer. However long you've been at it, you've started to question the choice or choices you've made up to now. In fact, if you've really given the matter some thought, you may be wondering whether you ever really *had* any choices. If that is your situation, you have plenty of company. After working for a while, many people start having qualms; they start asking themselves how they ended up where they are, and whether their daily routine is all they can expect to get out of a working life that can last thirty to forty years or more. Such questions may sometimes be based on a concern about money: There's too little of it for too much output of energy or too much boredom. But whether money enters into it or not, career-related doubts *always* have to do with job satisfaction.

You may feel that somewhere along the way you were hijacked by economic circumstances, or by what was "expected" of you. Some of you may be experiencing the phenomenon known as burnout. Or perhaps you now realize that what you chose as secure employment turned out to be boring employment. And these days, when employers who used to be regarded as stable, such as insurance companies, school districts, state and local governments, and major corporations, are being shaken to the roots by rapid societal and economic change, you may have come to the conclusion (correctly) that there is no such thing any more as a secure job.

This book demystifies the high-tech world, showing that there are all kinds of opportunities there for people like you. It's intended for nontechnical people who would like to move ahead, financially speaking, but who for various reasons feel that "high-tech," whatever the heck that is, is not a possibility for them. Through a little healthy irreverence, your attitude will change.

The book contains excerpts from dozens of interviews with other nontechies who are now working as professionals in high-tech enterprises around the United States. They'll give you a feeling for what it is really like to be in such a company. To say that it was fascinating listening to these men and women talk is to understate the case. The format was pretty open, though we had to have some structure, as my budget for cassettes was limited. I'll say nothing more about these wonderful people now, except that they really wrote the book (sorry, gang, no royalties for you!); you'll have no doubt that there can be a high-tech future for you after listening to them.

Chapter 3 tells you in detail how to plan and execute a high-tech job campaign. With a carefully planned and executed campaign plus a bit of luck, you can get what you want without killing yourself. And the process itself can be exciting and instructive. Before you can start such a campaign, however, you may have to face some internal (or, if you prefer, psychological) hurdles. These can be every bit as difficult to overcome as the external ones.

The first of these is a natural inertia that keeps you plodding along in the same old rut. Your work may not be satisfying, but it's what you know, and it makes no demands on you except stamina and a tolerance for the familiar. It may not pay well, but it's safe. It may be in a field that has little status, but you can comfort yourself that you, at least, can appreciate the real contribution it's making to building a better world. And somewhere down the line there is the prospect of retirement, perhaps on a pension plan of some kind. Then you can at last do what you really want!

This natural inertia often operates in combination with fear of change. Making a career move is risky, and, as I have observed, many people are risk-averse. What if you make the "wrong" move? What if you wake up a few months or years hence to the realization that the whole thing was an awful mistake—one that it is now too late to rectify?

What often shakes people out of their state of career inertia is the awareness that their career is not as safe as they thought it was when they started out. Teachers get fired. Actuaries get fired. So do salespeople, financial analysts, and in fact anyone who works for business or government. In fact, when you think about it, there really is no lifetime job security anymore, anywhere. So perhaps all of us should start at least thinking about alternatives to what we're doing today.

It's sad to realize that when people really do get fired, they often tend to expend a lot of time, money, and energy in a futile effort to get rehired into the same rut they were thrown out of. A friend of mine worked for twelve years in the field of architectual design. He is not an architect himself, but was involved in the marketing and sales side as a writer of many successful proposals for large architectural and urban planning and design projects. His employer was a large firm with over a hundred architects and a large backlog of work, so he was shocked when he lost his job late in 1990. The firm offered him some work under contract, which he was glad to accept, as it kept money flowing in. Instead of taking a hard look at where the architectural profession was going and why he had been let go (the management had correctly fore-seen that there would be a dearth of new large projects for several years), considering career alternatives, and taking whatever steps were neces-sary to recycle himself, he continued to do the same work he had done as a full-time employee. Except that now the work was sporadic, and eventually it petered out. When he finally saw what was happening, he used his contacts in the industry to do similar contract work for others. That work, too, ended. He is still unemployed and still knocking on the doors of a profession which, for the moment at least, appears moribund.

Another phenomenon that starts people thinking about career al-ternatives is burnout. The lawyer hasn't made partner; after years of slavery it is suggested that she perhaps start her own practice or try a move to another firm. The junior high school teacher is ready to toss in the towel after ten years in the trenches. The nurse has had it with irreg-ular shifts, low pay, and being looked down on by the doctors. And so it goes. Who doesn't know someone like this who is constantly saying that she or he is ready for a drastic change in work?

Another great motivator for being ready to contemplate a career change is the prospect of making more money. Social workers, for ex-ample, perform very important functions in our society. They work with some of the neediest members of our society, and we should honor them and reward them accordingly. But we do neither. We just expect them to soldier on at $18,000 a year. At that, they are better off than those we entrust with our children while we, the parents, are attending to our own lives. The turnover in workers at day-care centers is over 40 percent each year, not surprising when salaries in that area are in the lowest tenth for all wage earners.* But even when society accords respect to a profession, financial rewards don't necessarily follow. A friend of mine teaches English literature at a prestigious eastern college; in fact, he has an endowed chair. Getting it was quite an honor. But when I called him a few years ago on behalf of our alma mater's alumni fund-raising cam-paign, it was all I could do to get ten bucks out of him. Stingy? No, just budgeted down to the last penny.

I'm not suggesting that all underpaid social workers and college professors throw over their careers and try to move into the high-tech industry. All I'm suggesting is that they, and you, have choices. And I'm suggesting that if you feel burned out, or underpaid, or underval-ued, or simply ready for a change, you haul yourself out of the rut and seriously consider a change.

In Lewis Carroll's *Alice in Wonderland*, there's a great piece of advice:

The Spirit of Community: Rights, Responsibilities and the Communitarian Agenda, by Amitai Etzioni, Crown, 1993.

"Begin at the beginning, and go till you come to the end: then stop." That's how I suggest you read this book. I've assumed that you're currently unemployed, or at least underemployed, by which I really mean underpaid. And that you're looking to make a change. So the book begins by describing what the barriers are to your getting close to the high-tech world. You've got to appreciate these so that you don't spin your wheels trying the normal ways of getting a job—they just don't work in the high-tech industry. Then the book gives you some useful strategies for getting reliable information about job opportunities and job content. By strategies I mean things that will really work for you, and the book gets down to the nitty-gritty in this respect.

Lots of career books spend a lot of time on résumés. This one spends very little time on them—about as much as the average hiring manager does. On the other hand, you'll get a lot of ideas on networking, and it'll really pay you to listen to them. There are other techniques that have worked for nontechies, and the book goes into all of them. Once you've made it inside the walls, you're going to have to face a series of interviews, and the book explores this topic, too. You'll also learn what the human resources department does and doesn't do, and why you're really better off avoiding all contact with those folks at the beginning.

You've also got to know something about how high-tech industries are organized, because that is an important part of understanding how a job opportunity is situated within a company, what the chances are of promotion, and how easy it will be to make a lateral move into some other area of work. In this country high-tech companies are turning the old notion of moving up the corporate ladder on its side.

Chapter 4 is entitled "Computers in Ten Minutes." It'll be your start toward an understanding of computers, but more important, it will give you some idea of how absolutely fascinating and fast-moving the field is today. And it'll be your introduction to some of the jargon and buzzwords that will get you through your interviews in good style. (You don't have to use them yourself, just so long as you can understand them.)

Before you join any high-tech company, you'll want to know about its culture. Every company has one, and believe me, you don't want a job at any salary if you can't adapt to the culture. The only way to find out about it is to ask, and Chapter 5 tells you how to get the information you'll need to make an informed decision.

Once you are employed, you'll want to know how to "grow your job." This is easier in some places than in others, and is also easier for some people than for others. You've got to be reasonably happy at what you do, and expanding your responsibilities is one way of achieving this;

Chapter 6, "Thriving and Surviving," tells how. Trust me when I say that if you get into this field, you'll be living life in the fast lane most of your working day. You've got to know three things: how to stay employed regardless of shifts and swings in the industry, how to keep from being devoured by your job, and how to have fun and grow as a professional and as a human being. Fortunately, there are lots of wonderful ways of accomplishing these goals in the high-tech world.

Once you've got your feet wet and picked up some salable knowledge, you may find yourself dreaming of the magic world of startup companies. Chapter 7 gives you some information on what these are and how you can break into them. Some people start their careers in high-tech startups, and if everything works out right, they can end up being very, very, very rich. (Of course, I realize that you accord only a secondary importance to money income.)

High-tech products are a major export, and some companies offer opportunities for overseas work. Chapter 8, "Going International," explores both the upside and the downside of these jobs.

The book ends with a chapter entitled "Final Words of Wisdom." You'll know them when you get to them, so I won't reveal anything here.

Scott McNealy, who does not have a technical background, but didn't let that get in his way (he is now president and CEO of Sun Microsystems, Inc., a $5 billion computer company), told me what he believes it takes to succeed in the high-tech world. He said:

> You've got to have an intellectual curiosity. You've got to have a desire to make more than just money, you've got to want to improve the standard of living, the tools that we have, because that's what technology does. You're going to need some psychic income because it's hard work, but it's exciting. Sometimes I refer to it as too much chocolate cake.

Ready for some chocolate cake?

Blessed is he who has found his work;
let him ask no other blessedness.

—Carlyle

HI-TECH
JOBS
FOR
LO-TECH
PEOPLE

1

The Quest for the Job

A lot is being written these days about people having second, third, and even more careers. That's a great thing, because more and more people are realizing that they don't have to be trapped where they are today. They can empower themselves and change their lives from top to bottom if that's what it takes to make them happier human beings. This kind of change doesn't happen in some kind of magical way because you've attended a workshop on self-help, or empowerment, or whatever. But often that's a necessary first step, and if you really feel hemmed in and powerless to change things, you ought to investigate getting your head turned around. Sometimes people can get so immersed in what they're doing, trying to make sense of it and trying to survive while enjoying life a little, that they forget that they do have choices. They get hypnotized and end up staring straight ahead as they move through life. It's a lot easier to trudge along in a rut than it is to pull yourself out of it and find a new path. But some people reach a point where they stop for a moment to take their bearings and are open to new ideas, new directions. That's the point I hope you've reached, whether you've been working for three years or twenty-three years. Life is a marvelous cornucopia if you're willing to grab it and shake it a bit. You can do this out of a sense of adventure, or out of feelings of dissatisfaction and frustration with the course your life has taken up to now. If you are willing to contemplate new directions, I invite you to take a look at the world of high-tech industry.

What Is "High-Tech"?

What exactly *is* the high-tech industry? When the term is used in this book, it refers to the companies that perform research and development, manufacturing, and sales of computers, computer software, peripheral equipment, networks, communications, and related technology, as well as a myriad of associated publications and other services. There are lots of these companies, from tiny one- or two-person software development firms to multidivisional giants with tens of thousands of employees, and with worldwide operations and sales in the billions of dollars.

If there is one area of business in which the United States is clearly the world leader today, it is the high-tech industry. Though they have tried, the Japanese do not come close to having a leadership role in high tech. Nor do the Europeans. Taiwan and Korea are centers of efficient, relatively low-cost manufacturing, but they do little innovating. India is rapidly becoming a center for software development, and given unfettered access to world markets might become an effective competitor to the United States in this area, but this is at best several years away.

What Kinds of People Work in High Tech?

Because the know-how and products of the high-tech industry have an impact on so many other areas of our economy, it is terribly important for the economic health of the nation that the industry continue to grow. And it is growing. Yet many people contemplating a career change either do not consider a move to the high-tech industry or, if they do give the idea some thought, abandon it as impractical or too difficult to bring about. Those few who do make the transition to high tech usually do so at the urging and with the help of a friend who is already well established in it. Almost no one seems to make a deliberate decision to make the move, develop a plan, and then execute the plan. Certainly a central reason for this is the commonly held idea that the high-tech industry is for technical people—engineers or scientists, with maybe an occasional M.B.A. here and there to handle the business side of things. Nothing could be farther from the truth. Of course there are a lot of technical people in the industry. But that's not the whole story.

For those of you who have a background in the liberal arts and have had a rough time finding a really good, satisfying job, one that meets your expectations and challenges you to grow intellectually and emotionally, I have a really good piece of news: The high-tech industry *needs people like you!* That applies whether you've been working for only a few years or for many. Many of the people I met while researching this book were teachers or educational administrators, toiling in the trenches for years, working hours and dealing with situations that would put the toughest high-tech manager to shame. These people decided to make a change in their lives. They found that the high-tech industry offered them rewards, both financial and emotional, that were lacking or that had worn thin in their previous jobs. I've also met people who made the switch early in their working lives. I have met pianists who became programmers, and reporters who became salesmen; artists who became advertising managers and even electrical engineers; historians who are now product managers; and a woman who ran a gift shop for several years and is now an internal management consultant and trainer for a huge component manufacturer.

One of the things each of these people found when making this career change was a new self-esteem. Joining the high-tech industry is like joining an exclusive club, but what makes it exclusive is the quality of its members, its unique culture, and the admiration it evokes from the general public, rather than irrelevant issues of race, social status, or wealth. And as in the case of an exclusive club, it isn't easy to gain admission—but the difference is that you can control the process to a considerable extent, and make it happen *if you really want to*. Others have done it—why not you?

After almost twelve years working in it, I've become absolutely convinced that the high-tech industry is the most democratic there is. Once you are inside the walls, no one gives a damn about your degrees or your background. It can give you a completely fresh start in life—if that's what you want. I also found that the high-tech industry offers an opportunity to engage in—or, perhaps better, to indulge in—learning for the entire length of your working life. This learning is both informal and formal, with all expenses picked up by the employer. The industry is multicultural, both in its employees and in its products, as these have to be adapted for the various languages of the international marketplace. It is not uncommon in the industry to have in a single meeting employees with incredibly diverse ethnic backgrounds: Korean, Mexican, Anglo, African, Chinese, Indian, Polynesian—everyone from everywhere. What's important is performance and teamwork. It's the way the rest of society should be.

Are There Any Jobs Out There?

If you've read about all the layoffs that have recently decimated the ranks of some of the largest computer companies, you may be wondering how on earth I can have the gall to suggest that there are any jobs at all for folks like you out there. Aren't there thousands upon thousands of qualified people with many years' experience lined up waiting to try for the few openings that exist?

For every company that is downsizing in the high-tech industry, there are several that are upsizing. They aren't the big names that make the headline stories in the general news section, but they are serious, well-managed, growing enterprises. In the Boston area, for example, where such companies as DEC, Data General, Wang, and Prime have had to bite the bullet, if not the dust, a host of small software companies has sprung up. The vice-president of human resources of one of them made the surprising statement that "we just can't hire fast enough." I hadn't expected to hear that, but a glance at the Classified section of the Sunday *Boston Globe* confirmed that there was indeed a lot of hiring activity under way just when people were writing off this part of the country as a hopeless casualty of the recession.

In fact, most high-tech companies seem to be growing these days, as the *San Jose Mercury News* reported back in April 1993:

> While the rest of the country struggles with the aftermath of recession, the capital of American technology has come roaring back. By every measure, Silicon Valley's largest companies appear to be in robust health and competing very effectively.
>
> At the same time, tremendous growth in the number of smaller, newly public companies in the area suggests that Silicon Valley has moved quickly to take advantage of new opportunities and is well positioned to benefit from emerging technologies.*

Even companies that have laid off huge percentages of their workforces are doing some hiring. In some cases this is for very narrowly defined technical positions, but in others there are actually openings in nontechnical positions similar to those that were vacated through layoffs. How can this be? There's a normal process of attrition at work. People leave one area and move to another. Employees start businesses of their own, or join a startup. Certainly in a period of economic recession the attrition rate slows down, but it doesn't stop. And what about competition from those who were laid off? Often they don't find out about the opportunity—they are in no better position than you are when it comes to that, unless the opening is in the company they were with. Even then, they may not wish to take the position; it may be at a lower level than their former job and they don't want to take a step backwards.

If the opening is at another company, job seekers who come from the industry may run into some problems you won't have. They may encounter a prejudice, and it can be strong, against outsiders who have been doing much the same kind of job at other companies. If they did it

*BusinessMonday, *San Jose Mercury News*, April 12, 1993.

so well, how come their company is in the pits? If it isn't in the pits, how come they want to leave it? There may also be cultural issues: We are Company X, and we are a fast-moving, street-smart bunch of gut-punching workaholics. Here comes this job applicant from Company Y in her power suit and gold-laminated resumé who thinks she can fit into our team. Preposterous!

It's strange that all this should be so, but the high-tech industry is, for all its mystique, a very human institution. People do things for other people because they like them, because they did their homework and presented their case well, because they were persistent and persuasive. You will be at no disadvantage in these respects.

How Hard Is It to Get a High-Tech Job?

*Rich's High Tech Business Guide,** a valuable research tool that is available at some libraries, gives the following numbers of high-tech companies in different regions of the country:

Pacific Northwest	2,300
Texas	2,600
Rocky Mountains	3,000
Massachusetts	3,073
Maine/Vermont/New Hampshire	1,257
Connecticut/Rhode Island	1,712
Southern California	5,600
Silicon Valley/Northern California	7,467

The *Technology Resource Guide*[†] for 1993, another immensely useful resource for those who want to learn about high-tech companies, reported that "emerging technology" companies employing less than 1,000 people predicted a growth of almost 13,000 new jobs in computer hardware, 21,500 in software, and 10,600 in computer assemblies and components for the next twelve months. These numbers do not include jobs that become available through attrition, nor do they consider the plans of larger companies. And this is in an era of severe economic recession, from which the economy is now emerging.

If you are interested in a change, the high-tech industry has something to offer you.

*Rich's High Tech Business Guide to Silicon Valley and Northern California, Rich's Business Directories, Inc., 1992. Other editions cover the first seven areas listed. A small number of medical technology firms are included in these figures.
[†]Corporate Technology Information Services, Inc., 1993.

2

The Jobs

I asked an experienced management trainer at a large computer company what jobs could be handled by people with a nontechnical background. Her comments are encouraging:

> Actually, it's quite open. As long as you have access to experts, meaning the folks that are technical, and you know how to communicate with them and you know whom to contact, you should be able to do most jobs.

The only jobs that are absolutely closed to people with a nontechnical background are the R&D positions. Unless you are a self-taught genius, you simply won't be able to design integrated circuits or complex software without having put in a few years of formal study. And some of the professional positions are similarly closed unless you have the right ticket. You can't get on the corporate legal staff, for example, unless you can wave your law degree around. Similarly, some finance jobs will require that you be a CPA, or that you have an M.B.A. and a command of international tax questions. And so forth.

But everything else is possible. Sure, you won't sail into many of these positions without gearing up for them. You have to go about it in the right way, and with patience. And that's a good thing, because getting there is more than half the fun; it involves a whole process of self-discovery and development, plus the joyful amazement when you realize that you've moved into a totally new working life, and that you like it and it likes you. We'll look at what this voyage involves in the next chapter. Right now let's look more closely at the sorts of jobs you might consider.

When I started thinking about this topic, I thought that presenting it to you would be a breeze. I felt that all jobs in the high-tech industry could rather easily be divided into "hard-tech" and "soft." The hard-tech jobs would have to do with the guts of the hardware and software, whether it was designing, building, or repairing them. The soft jobs would be those being done by people who didn't have technical degrees. But as I started to interview lots of people in the industry, I realized that things were not so straightforward.

First, I was amazed at how the soft jobs in high tech are related to the technology and its evolution. People occupying such positions often describe themselves in a somewhat self-deprecating way as "nontechnical," and perhaps that is true in the sense that they have had no formal technical training. But everything is relative, and it is quite apparent that many—indeed most—of the people I interviewed for this book had learned a lot about the technical aspects of their company's products. In fact, they had had to do so in order to do their jobs well. Take the job of public relations. If your image of such people is one of flacks who are hired to grind out whatever material will induce people to buy a product, you haven't met a PR person working in the high-tech industry. He or she works on a team where everyone is expected to get up to speed on the products: What they do, their positioning with respect to the needs out in the marketplace, and what the competition is doing.

The second thing that surprised me was how many people there were in admittedly technical positions who had nontechnical backgrounds. Some of them had no college degree at all. Perhaps that ought not to have been such a surprise. After all, this is the industry of Bill Gates, who dropped out of college to build a software empire out of Microsoft, and to become along the way the richest man in America. But I wasn't prepared for the young man who was the product manager in a large company for a very technical product and whose college education had been almost entirely in the field of history. His specialty, in fact, was early Church history. He got into it because he didn't like crowds.

> I thought I wanted to go into science, but in the first quarter
> you had to take basic chemistry. The class was the size of my
> entire high school—1,600 students in four sections of 400 stu-
> dents each. Needless to say, I soon switched my major!

Or the man who majored in Sanskrit studies (I'm not making this up) who also ended up in product management. Or the woman who had a degree in fashion design and marketing, got tired of dealing with fabrics, got into a hardware sales training program a few years ago, and now pulls down about $130,000 a year helping an international banking organization make sense of its computing systems. Or the former small retailer with no college degree but a considerable talent in graphic art who deals every day with software development engineers and creates successful ad campaigns.

So here was a paradox! The lack of a technical education didn't prevent these and many, many other people from getting jobs in the high-tech industry, yet when you really took a look at what they were doing, they had achieved a considerable (and, to my eyes, overwhelming) command of the technology. In some cases they had had to do so; in others they had chosen to do so as a way of growing their jobs and making themselves more valuable. And in a rather heartening number of cases, they had done so because they just got fascinated and found it was pretty easy. One thing became apparent: One couldn't blithely classify jobs as technical or nontechnical, and simply encourage and coach people to apply for the nontechnical ones. To a degree all jobs had some technical aspects.

Let's make it clear that when we talk about technological aspects of traditionally nontechnological jobs, we're talking about high-level technology. Chances are that unless you're a genius, without a degree in technology, you'll never design an ASIC, or application-specific integrated circuit. But you *will* be able to know what the term means and use it intelligently in discussions with engineers, salespeople, or whomever. You may not understand precisely how multitasking operates, but if you know that it keeps your computer screen from freezing up so that you can't move on to another operation until the earlier process has finished, you're on your way to achieving a high-level understanding of the technology. You gain tremendous respect for the women and men who dream up and develop this stuff, sure. But the wonderful, mind-blowing thing is that you gain new respect for yourself (not to mention from your friends) when one day, not too long after starting your high-tech job, you wake up and start to understand it. Achieving high-level knowledge of technology not only is not difficult, it's actually fun. As a friend of mine put it, "My God! I think I need professional help—this stuff is starting to make sense to me!"

Faced with a confusing taxonomic problem, I decided to present you with a very simple alphabetical list of activities that take place in high-tech and that are usually carried out by nontechnical people. It'll give you some idea of the breadth of possibilities. It's not intended to be exhaustive because there are many possible permutations and combinations. Some companies use different names for the same function. And please don't worry if you don't find an exact match between what you've been doing for the past few years and these activities; the idea at this stage is to pique your interest, not to consummate the marriage.

The descriptions also give readers a good idea of all the activities that occur in a high-tech company. I haven't included general management, because true general management in the high-tech industry really tends to occur only at the vice-presidential level, and I assume you won't start your career as a VP. I did include president, though—I just couldn't resist.

Here's my list, followed by a description of each activity. (Some of the activities shown under marketing are sometimes found somewhere else in the high-tech company.)

Account management
Administrator
Contract negotiations
Contract administration
Customer education and training
Customer service representative
Customer service business manager
Customer response center
Forecasting (orders and shipments)
Human resources management
Independent software vendor (ISV) relations
Marketing
   Advertising
   Catalog design and publication
   Channels communication
   Channels management
   Channels recruitment
   Channels sales support
   Channels sales training
   Channels technical training
   Conferences and seminars
   Demand creation
   Field sales communication
   Marketing communications
   Product inquiries
   Product marketing
   Product packaging
   Product pricing
   Public relations
   Sales kit preparation
Operations
Order operations
President
Project management
Publications management

Sales
Sales support
Systems administrator
Technical editing and publishing
Technical writing
Telesales
Training
Training management

When you are networking to find a job in the high-tech industry, which you'll learn how to do in Chapter 3, you should see if the positions you hear about match, or sound like, the ones on this list. In the rest of this chapter I'll give you a brief description of many of these positions as they are generally understood in the high-tech industry. Not only will this add to your understanding of the positions, it will also give you a better idea of what working in the industry actually entails. I haven't described all of the positions, because some are self-explanatory.

Account Management

Account management, sometimes called large or national account management, is usually a responsibility given to someone who has been working in the company for a few years. Generally speaking, it does not require deep technical knowledge. This function really involves giving the most important customers a single point of contact within the company for the resolution of business issues. What is most important is that the customer feel that someone in the high-tech company is dedicated to making the relationship work well, and is always available by phone or fax. Being responsive is the key to success as an account manager.

This function also gives the senior sales management of the high-tech company—the directors or vice-presidents of sales and finance are usually the ones most concerned—an unbiased view of how relations between the company and its customer are evolving. The view is unbiased in the sense that the account manager's salary is usually not tied to quarterly sales numbers. Thus his or her recommendations to management regarding all aspects of the relationship are more likely to reflect a concern for the long term. Sales representatives may actually have more frequent contact with the customer, but this contact is aimed exclusively at achieving quarterly sales goals. If a sales rep is having trouble making his numbers, he may devise schemes for accomplishing this that will serve him personally quite well in the short term, but that may adversely affect the company-customer relationship over a period of time. An example would be to sell a large quantity of a certain item that the sales rep has reason to believe may be going EOL* in a few weeks. Since high-tech customers do not like to get stuck with obsolete goods, and usually insist on returning them anyway, in such a case the account manager might work with the customer and the sales rep and his boss to arrange an easy transition from the old product to the new, perhaps planning for a low- or no-cost upgrade.

The account manager usually has contact with a higher level of management than does the sales rep, though this is not always the case.

Account management is considered a headquarters function, but in fact the people who carry it out are sometimes located not at headquarters but at the regional sales office closest to the customer's corporate headquarters.

Account management often requires some travel, because large customers may have several locations throughout the country, or even overseas, where various important issues may arise, the resolution of which calls for the participation of local people.

Account managers are sometimes recruited from the industry they will deal with as an employee of the high-tech company. Thus, someone from the oil and gas industry who knows its data processing needs may end up working for a high-tech company as an account manager for one or more oil companies. Alternatively, sometimes assignments are made on a geographical basis—an account manager may take responsibility for three or four major accounts in the Pacific Northwest, for example, and these accounts may be in quite unrelated industries.

Administrator

The position of administrator is of considerable interest to nontechnical people, since getting hired into it is relatively easy. On the surface, administrators† may seem to do for high-tech companies what secretaries do for other companies. In fact, though, the positions can be quite different. The traditional secretary has a boss; the administrator is a member of (and "supports") a team or workgroup. Some admins (the short term by which those occupying the position are almost exclusively known) might complain that they have not one but several "bosses."

---

*EOL stands for "end of life." When a product is EOL'd, it is withdrawn from the price list; that is, it is no longer available for sale. Occasionally the sales force isn't informed in time and keeps selling it.

†The name of the position can vary from one company to another; for example, in Apple such persons are known as area associates.

The high-tech company doesn't have some of the tasks that secretaries carry out in other industries. For example, almost no one in high-tech ever writes a letter. Communication is carried on by phone, E-mail, or fax, all of which can be done directly from a manager's or individual contributor's desk. When letters are required, they are almost always written by the sender on a computer and either printed out directly or sent to the admin for printing out on company stationery. Appointments can be made by computer over the network, and since high-tech managers and others can consult one another's appointment calendars in this way, the admin's intervention is often not necessary. But some routine tasks almost always account for a large part of the admin's working day. These vary, but may include arranging customer visits, setting up large meetings, arranging travel for members of the workgroup, preparing overheads for presentations, delivering interoffice mail, working at trade shows, arranging for supplies, setting up lunches and customer visits, and so forth. Admins may support a single person (for example, a senior manager), but are more often found supporting ten or even more people.

In the best high-tech environments (at least, best for the administrator), he or she is accorded considerable scope and flexibility concerning *how* to support the others in the workgroup, and the person to whom the admin reports (and thus, his or her de facto "boss") will assist him or her in getting involved with projects. The admin may perform research, for example, to assist with a particular project.

The major dividing line between the admin and the other members of the team is that the admin is an hourly, nonexempt employee. Another is that admins are located in workspaces that look different from others; it is rare for an admin to have a closed office, for example. The position has served some people very well (admin jobs can pay up to $50,000 a year in some cases), and some admins are very pleased with what they are doing. But some are not, and when an entry-level job within a professional category opens up, it is usual to have several admins trying for the position.

The issue of the status of the admin job, like that of the secretary in other industries, has provoked some heated controversy. Some admins feel that they are overqualified for the job—for example by virtue of education—and that not only do they deserve to be treated with more "respect," but they should be helped to move out of the job into an entry-level salaried job as soon as possible. But good admins are hard to find, and a person who feels overqualified may find herself locked into the position if she does a good job. I interviewed people for this book who started as admins and became professionals very quickly; I've also known some who quit in frustration.

Contract Administration

This one sounds clunky, doesn't it? Paper pushing, filing, yawning from time to time. Yet the terms governing sales, service, and financial relationships between high-tech companies and their most important customers are not left to the whims of a sales rep. They are all carefully defined by contract. At least, an attempt is made to define them carefully. Lawyers work hard to get the perfect contract, which means, of course, perfect from the point of view of the seller, the high-tech enterprise. With luck the customer will sign it as is, but that kind of luck is generally reserved for people who win the lottery. Usually the customer has its own ideas about what will make the relationship fly. Companies such as Boeing, Exxon, Pepsico, Bell South, and American Express have lawyers of their own, after all. By the time these folks get through with the basic agreement, it may have all kinds of special terms written into it.

It is the contract administrator's job to know the terms of the contract cold and to manage the execution of the contract. The relations between the parties established by the contract aren't static; the contract calls for each side to take various actions over a period of time, and provides for remedies should things start to go awry. An example is the area of product warranties. Customers want the products they buy to be trouble-free, and if there is trouble, they want to know that the manufacturer or vendor or both will stand behind the product. In the high-tech world, new products come out every year and a half or sooner, and they are immensely complex. Things do tend to go wrong, and sometimes there is a question as to whether a particular case is covered and what the contractual remedy is. The contract administrator can advise the sales and service people what the contract has provided. Sometimes she plays a direct role in negotiating disagreements. To do this, she may have to visit the customer for discussions, set up meetings involving technical, legal, or business personnel, and sometimes recommend that the contract be rewritten to take account of new business realities.

Contracts usually have an expiration date, and it is also the administrator's job to keep track of this and send out the proper notices for renewal where that is desired. Other people in the company have to be informed of the termination of a contract; it is awkward for the contract to have expired (or, worse, been intentionally terminated by the parties) and to have business continue as before, carried on by unwitting sales or other personnel.

Customer Education and Training

This function involves training those who buy a company's products how to use or maintain them. Some large companies that have in-house training and education departments will offer one set of courses to customers and another to their own employees. These two sets of courses may cover similar topics, but because of a desire to keep some aspects of a product or process confidential or for other reasons, there will be some slight differences between them. Courses for users are usually nontechnical, and therefore training departments don't require that the people presenting them have a technical background.

What is important is having "platform" (i.e., teaching) skills, being articulate, and being able to present the material in an interesting way. Almost anyone with these skills who has also acquired a good command of the company's products can be taken seriously as a potential trainer.

An allied activity is that of course developer. There are degree and certificate programs in course development, and nontechnical people who meet the basic qualifications for being a trainer can move to the developer position rather easily by taking an after-hours program.

High-tech companies usually present such courses in their own facilities, simply because that is the easiest way of satisfying the equipment requirements; user courses require a system for each student, sometimes a local area network, servers, overhead projectors, audiovisual equipment, and so forth. The companies may also rely to a degree on outside contractors (individuals) for presenting courses.

Customer Service Representative

The customer service (CS) function has been one of the channels by which nontechnical people have moved into and up in the high-tech industry. Customer service includes everything the high-tech company provides, or is prepared to provide, after the sale of its products. In some companies the list of services for hardware and software is long, including warranty service, sale of upgrades and spare parts, service contracts, training, consulting, "hot lines," and, where the company decides to provide some of these functions through an outside contractor, the management of third parties.

It's been said that the sales department lives with the customer only up to the moment of the sale; the customer service department lives with the customer forever. Certainly a large part of a high-tech company's reputation in the market depends on the market's perception of the range and quality of its service. In fact, customer service is rapidly becoming an important market "differentiator" between companies; because of this, high-tech companies are investing more in this area, which means there are better chances of job openings.

There is still a debate going on in the industry as to whether CS should be a cost center or a profit center. Being a cost center means that everything the CS department does (or most of it) is subsidized by the sales function. For example, the sales department might be required to kick in 2 percent of its revenues to fund after-sale service. Being a profit center means that the service department is run like an independent business. The company has invested in it and wants a good return on its investment—as good a return as from any other part of the company.

It's always better to be part of a CS group that is run like an independent business, because such a group charges directly for its services, and tends to be sharper and more responsive; also, you are very close to the customer (excellent for learning, and for survival when times get tough and "excess" employees are at risk), and you can really learn how a business is run. CS groups that are well managed tend to have a high level of esprit de corps, perhaps because in many companies they are understaffed and overworked, and depend on their morale and energy to carry the day. CS is a sort of U.S. Marine Corps of high tech; everyone depends on it and at the same time beats up on it. As in the USMC, the level of professionalism in CS tends to be very high. The generic name I've given to entry- and midlevel positions in CS is customer service representative, but there are many sorts of jobs within this department. The entry-level positions for nontechnical people usually involve manning the first line of contact with customers (i.e, the phones), doing contract administration, or even doing clerical work. The mobility within CS is high, and it is possible to move up within the organization or outside to a hardware or software sales position after gaining a range of experience in the CS department.

Customer Service Business Manager

This person runs the profit-oriented customer service function as an independent business within the high-tech company. The position is usually very well paid, and may be at the director level. Several years of experience inside the CS group is an absolute prerequisite for moving into this position; ideally, the CS business manager would also have a business degree (which one can acquire at company expense). But it is not necessary to have an education in technology; you can acquire the requisite knowledge along the way.

The CS business manager usually has a number of technical people reporting to him or her. Whether rightly or wrongly, in many companies, technical service people have the reputation of being cantankerous and hard to manage. And the CS department often deals with customers who are unhappy because of system, software, or network problems. The best CS managers therefore have excellent people skills, as well as an in-depth knowledge of the very specialized CS business.

Customer Response Center

This also involves dealing with people over the telephone, but this time they are calling you with questions about your company's products. The response center in this case is located not in CS, but in the marketing or sales department. These calls usually don't involve complaints. Instead, they seek information. Sometimes this gets into quite technical areas, but the joy of it is that the caller almost never expects a quick answer. You can concentrate on getting the question down correctly, getting the caller's name and phone number, and committing to call back within an agreed time with at least an interim response. Then you go and get the answer from the right person. (The company does not keep you chained to the phone.) The beauty of this kind of work is that, as in telesales and in the customer service function, you are dealing with customers or partners outside the company. It is very helpful to have experience involving customer contact on your resumé. Customers really are the most important people in the world when you're in business, and business people, including hiring managers, value people who have dealt with customers successfully. In a customer response center position, you learn who and where the internal technical resources of the company are and build relationships with these people. You also build your technical understanding day by day, and though this may be imperceptible at the start and you may think you are just relaying information blindly from one person to another, the day will come when you will suddenly realize that you know the answer to the caller's question. You don't have to go bother your friend in product engineering, as nice as he's been about it up to now. In a few months you will know a lot, and you'll know that you know it. Time to update the resumé again by including the technical knowledge and people skills you've been building up.

Sometimes persons outside the high-tech industry hesitate to get involved with any job involving the telephone. It seems to be too low-status. Well, listen to the words of a woman who's been doing this kind of work for a few months at a software company, and who got her position through an agency:

> Actually I wasn't interested in the position. But they encouraged me to come here and interview for the position, because I might change my mind. And that was true, because once I found out more about what I'd be doing and I met the people,

I thought maybe it would work out for me in the long run. At first I thought I was going to be answering questions eight hours a day. It turns out that I do that about 25 percent of the time. A lot of the callers ask me, How does this work? A lot of the time I don't know, but I'm reading all the spec sheets and trying to understand it as much as possible. And because I'm hearing it so much, I'm learning it. And if no one in the group knows the answer, I have to go to an engineer. It'll take a while, because I haven't had any formal training on it.

I've had a chance to learn about the workstation and the applications, and that's very useful anywhere. I can allocate an hour or two a day to myself for learning. And I'm doing some other projects as well.

Telephone jobs are good springboards to other positions in the high-tech company and are natural places to start growing your job using the techniques described in Chapter 6.

Forecasting (Orders and Shipments)

Forecasting is the means by which companies seek to synchronize the supply of goods with the market demand for those goods. There is usually a small group of people charged with this responsibility.

If one is selling toothpaste, synchronizing production with demand isn't much of a problem, since both the characteristics of the product and the demand for it remain fairly stable over time; you can look at historical sales numbers and pretty well predict the future. But if one is selling a high-tech product (a workstation, for example), the product may have a life cycle of only a few months before a newer product moves into the same market space. This complicates the forecasting task, because historical sales numbers may be no guide at all to what is going to happen in the future. High-tech companies rely to some degree on the past, but even more on what their customers tell them they want and plan to buy. Customers may inform the company that they need a workstation that sells for a certain price, and that if they can get it at that price, they will buy hundreds or thousands. If they can't get such a product, then they might say they'll be buying PCs with black-and-white monitors, but at a much cheaper price.

If this information is obtained from large, reliable customers and the manufacturer is planning to come out with a workstation at the right price, sales volumes can be estimated. A member of a forecasting group describes how it works in practice:

We would look at a few things. One was historically what we'd been selling at various price points. We'd divide our product line into four different price points for simplification. We'd look at requirements as reported by our sales force. And then we'd look at our own product rollout plan, talking to engineering and operations people. It's very much an art because of the kind of business we're in. It requires a quite extensive understanding of the product. There's a lot of uncertainty in it.

Forecasting can be critical to the success of the company when there are shortages of the components used to make the product, and hence long lead times for ordering them. A few years ago a major computer company underestimated demand for a new machine and, as a result of a shortage of monitors from a supplier, found itself with a huge backlog of orders. Luckily for the company, most of its customers stuck with it and waited for some months before getting the systems. The risk is that customers will become angry at the delay and buy someone else's systems.

It is not necessary to have a technical degree to be a good forecaster, but you do need to know your company's product line and understand some of the dynamics of the market. Companies tend to favor people with business degrees for forecasting positions. These positions get those in them good exposure to the engineering, sales, and marketing departments, as well as to top management. If forecasts are significantly off, factories will be making the wrong product mix, or too few or too many of a given product; the purchasing department may likewise under- or overestimate the company's requirements. So it is an important assignment.

Human Resources

Probably no professional area has been subject to so much criticism and experienced so much turmoil in recent years as the human resources (HR) function. This is due partly to the way this function was usually staffed, particularly at the lower levels, and partly to the economic squeeze placed on many large high-tech companies by declining profit margins in the hardware business. Yet it is a critical function within a company, since, in the high-tech industry, human resources usually represent the biggest single cost. It can offer a real career challenge to articulate nontechnical people with training and experience in effective communications, psychology, educational management, and other fields. In considering a career in high-tech HR, you should be aware of some recent history.

In the high-tech industry, human resources was traditionally an area where admins, secretaries, and clerical staff had a chance to move on to the first step of the salaried employee ladder. HR generalist was the generic title for such entry-level positions, which dealt with the administration of benefits and compensation plans, tracking of employee records, and so forth. These sorts of activities are the technical part of the HR function. They don't require a great deal of creativity or higher education, and so they were highly desired by low-level hourly employees. One of the problems this situation engendered was that as companies grew rapidly in the 1980s, HR departments also grew, and following the general rule of promoting from within, many HR departments promoted people out of the technical side of the function into managerial and professional positions. Some of the people thus promoted had already acquired the necessary training by attending courses and seminars, and were able to make the transition successfully. Many, however, simply found themselves out of their element—promoted too high, with decision-making power and with responsibility for managing others, but with no training in how to perform these functions.

In an industry where top managers were prone to make statements such as "our employees are our most important assets" or "the only real asset this company has is its workforce," and where the HR department was putatively in charge of employee welfare, a gap rapidly grew up between employees' expectations of HR and what the department was able to provide. A typical comment from an employee describes the situation:

> A minor part of their job should be administration, yet that seems to be a major part of their program. They don't have consulting skills, they don't have change management skills, they don't know how to do those things.

But in the 1980s many high-tech companies were making so much money that it was fairly easy to keep employees contented through generous raises every year and other rewards, such as bonuses. In the 1990s, as economic times turned sour, companies turned off the tap; raises became smaller, and nonpecuniary recognition became the way good performance was rewarded. Some departments reduced their staffing, and for the first time in many years employees became aware that they did not have guaranteed lifetime jobs with the company, as can be seen by these remarks from an executive who has spent twenty years in HR:

The role of HR has evolved in the time I've been associated with it. In the early years you took on a role to ensure that the people assets were managed as fairly and equitably as the capital assets of the company, that their views were represented and that they were taken into account. . . . In the competitive environment we're in today, jobs are at risk, and therefore your job is to ensure that the interests of the majority of the enterprise are looked after. If that necessitates a reduction in force, then that is achieved in a fair manner.

HR includes a very important area usually called employee communications. This encompasses everything from seeing that decisions of top management are conveyed to the workforce through announcements, newsletters, and the like, to providing a channel for airing of grievances, including possible violations of employees' rights. Another important area is employee training and development. Training departments usually come under the HR umbrella; training is considered separately in this chapter.

ISV Relations

ISV stands for independent software vendor. ISVs are of capital importance because they create the applications software that businesses actually use to solve problems. To track their accounts receivable, inventory, and payroll, for example, large retail chains use software that some ISV developed and that the chains bought. Maybe they bought it directly from the developer (the ISV), maybe they bought it through a systems integrator that managed the installation of their total information management system, or maybe they bought it as a package deal with the hardware. It's a fact of life that a computer without applications that will run on it is just a useless hunk of iron. And that being the case, it's awfully nice for the retailer to know that the software it bought to run its business is compatible with the hardware and the operating system.

There are thousands of ISVs out there developing applications software, some one- or two-person firms, and some with hundreds of employees. The computer companies pay them a lot of attention because they want all that software to run on their computers, or no one will *buy* their computers. So hardware companies and their divisions that develop operating systems try to work closely with the software developers to get them to develop or port their software (usually referred to in the industry as "solutions") to the companies' particular machines (usually referred to as "platforms"). Microsoft, a giant in the software industry, owns the fantastically popular MS-DOS operating system, currently in its sixth iteration, as well as the new NT operating system. Microsoft has no trouble attracting most ISVs for the very simple reason that just about every PC in the world runs on MS-DOS, and that's a big software market for the ISVs to shoot at. Volume is the name of the game for the ISVs.

It is not necessary to have a technical background to work in this field. People who work in ISV relations work closely with the software applications companies, line them up for industry trade shows (to showcase the software capabilities on the machines), get them to participate in important customer visits, and are the point of contact for all sorts of business-related issues. They play a key role in coordinating efforts to get the ISV to port to the company's operating system, a consummation so devoutly to be wished that to help out with the port, companies will lend engineers to ISVs (who may have a fabulous piece of software, but may be a tiny outfit with only a few people). A port may require both manpower and money, and for applications deemed critical, a large company may fork over a lot of money to "buy the port."

The larger ISVs themselves, of course, have a similar need to manage *their* relations with the large hardware and software companies, and again these positions are available to the nontechnical person.

Marketing

Few people seem to be able to define exactly what "marketing" means, yet every nontechnical person and many technical people in the high-tech industry seem to want a job doing it. What exactly is marketing in the high-tech context? One person described it thus:

> Marketing is doing everything you have to do to sell the product except actually getting out there and selling it.

In case that wasn't entirely helpful, here's a story—from a marketing manager at a small instrument company—of a whizbang product developed by a team of top engineers at a startup company, but *without* the benefit of any input from marketing. It demonstrates the importance of marketing activities *before* a product is even developed:

> Well, this new product line was considered the hardware designers' dream product. It never got going. It was a classic failure. It totally derailed the company, big time. You've got to look at the market requirements; you create a specification, and you try to build something the market wants. If you leave

it to the engineers, they go, 'Wow! If I can put this and this together, I can make this! And then everyone will come running to my door.' The better mousetrap thing. No marketing input, no research, just engineers' dreams. It ate up all our venture funding and all the profits.

One of the important tasks of the marketing organization is to make sure that the company is aware of and responds to the needs of the marketplace, not of its technical staff.

Incidentally, the person who recounted the above tale of woe is now the marketing manager of the startup company, which, though small, is now highly profitable. This person's preparation for the world of high tech consisted of an undergraduate degree in psychology with a minor in philosophy, a love of writing, and an ability to type really fast "from having to do all those papers."

As can be seen by the list at the beginning of this chapter, the marketing function is composed of a myriad of activities, all of which pres-

The "better mousetrap" thing.

ent opportunities for the nontechnical person. The traditional business school jargon describes marketing as consisting of the four p's—product, pricing, promotion, and placement. Sometimes a fifth p is added, for positioning. In planning new products, it's not enough to know what the market wants; you have to keep an eye on how the competition is seeking to meet these needs by introducing its own products—Company A will try to position its new offerings to edge out the competition in terms of price-performance, or some other criterion. If the market wants a laptop computer with certain technical characteristics, and Company A's competitors have already introduced some in a certain price range, it won't do Company A much good to introduce its own laptop at a slightly higher price. So being in marketing can be like playing a game, where you try to outguess and outplay your competition.

In addition to these activities, marketing people can be members of various committees dealing with business policy and tactical issues.

Some marketing activities, such as advertising, product packaging, and preparation of catalogs, are almost identical to those with the same name found outside the high-tech industry. If there's any difference, it's that the high-tech practitioner needs to have more product knowledge than his or her counterparts in other industries. That is because the features and benefits of high-tech products are more complex than, for example, those of a new soap powder or cereal. So acquiring some real product knowledge is important. I have not offered a description of these activities.

Other marketing activities in high tech are quite a bit different from similar activities in other industries. An example is the way sales channels* are used to get the products into the hands of end users. High-tech channels are affected by rapid changes in the marketplace and in the technology, just as the producers of hardware and software are themselves. This puts a premium on good management of the channels. In some companies the channels function comes under sales, in others under marketing. Both departments deal with channels intensively. Many nontechnical people can be found doing channels-related work in the high-tech industry.

Many discrete activities come under the general heading of channels management. These include channels communication, recruitment, sales support, sales training, and technical training. These are all self-explanatory once you get an idea of what the various types of high-tech channels are and how the hardware or software manufacturer relates to them.

*Channels are independent companies used as intermediaries to get a product to market. They are discussed in the next section.

Channels Management

Channels are independent companies that the high-tech manufacturer contracts with to help get its products to the end users. Channels can be of various types; master distributors, distributors, value-added resellers (VARs), and original equipment manufacturers (OEMs) are common ones.

What is the importance of channels in the high-tech industry? Some high-tech companies sell directly to customers because their products are very expensive and low-volume, so it's worth their having an in-house sales force. And the same may be true when products cost only a few thousand dollars each, but a potential customer may be considering buying a thousand of them. There are some advantages in having products sold by an in-house group. For one thing, there's more control over the whole complex sales process. Selling high-tech products isn't just a matter of providing some brochures, putting on a presentation, quoting a price, and asking for the order. It's a process that can last for months, and it may involve dealing with many different levels and functions within the customer's organization—MIS (management information systems) directors, financial officers, purchasing agents, technical staff. The competitors aren't sitting back, either. Each of them is having a go at the sales prospect, boosting its products, and spreading FUD (fear, uncertainty, and doubt) about the others'. So for big deals most high-tech companies would prefer to exercise as much control over the selling process as possible.

But in the real world it often isn't possible. Customers are many and dispersed all over the country, indeed, all over the globe. Direct sales is very expensive. Many high-tech companies just can't afford to have the coverage, in terms of "feet on the street," that is necessary to be successful. The independent companies that act as sales channels offer the opportunity to vastly increase the number of sales personnel selling the company's products, because such channels have their own sales forces. Furthermore, even if a high-tech company has large numbers of really good salespeople on board, all of whom are well versed in the products, it is simply impossible for them to know all they would have to know about the special needs of all their potential customers. Customers for high-tech products are in areas as complex and diverse as railroad operation, tax administration, forestry management, university administration, and management of telephone networks. Such customers expect potential suppliers to have more than a layman's understanding of their particular industry. They will do business with salespeople who demonstrate a real knowledge of the problems they're trying to solve. Some channels do have special understanding of some market segments, and this is an efficient way for companies to sell into these segments without having to learn all about how they operate.

Thus the high-tech industry relies on sales channels to get a multiplier effect—to multiply the number of salespeople representing its products; it also uses them to implement marketing programs and to sell into situations where customers want a mix of products and services. Where the channel has some special expertise—say in the oil industry—the high-tech manufacturer can use the channel to achieve credibility in that industry. Channels are usually required to carry inventory, thus relieving the manufacturer of this burden. Services, too, such as repairs, spare parts, and customer training, are often provided through channels. The creation and maintenance of an effective channels system is increasingly a major part of the activity of most large high-tech organizations. Inquiring of someone inside the high-tech company about its channels organization may yield the information that it is scheduled to expand.

This system has to be managed by people who have good business sense and who can communicate effectively by telephone, by fax, and in person. Channels have to be well managed because they are now representing the company, and to the degree they are used, the company's fate is in their hands. It is not necessary to have a technical degree to work in channels management; it is necessary to know the company's product line and its plans for new products, and to have excellent business sense.

Here are the various types of channels used by the high-tech industry.

OEMs

OEM stands for original equipment manufacturer. These are companies that buy the high-tech company's product and incorporate it into something that they make. The OEM then sells that product to an end user. An example is a flight simulator, which airlines use to train pilots without risking their airplanes at the same time. Flight simulators have computers in them, but no one sees the computers except the service personnel, who may occasionally have to take a look and give them a squirt of oil.* Another example is your telephone company, which may at this moment be bidding to upgrade the phone system of some underdeveloped country. The switching system your phone company is bidding may contain computers, but no one knows or cares about them so long as the calls get through. Some of these OEMs may be giants such

*Just kidding. You don't really oil them.

as AT&T; others may be small startups with a great new technology that they are just starting to bring to market. The role of channels management may vary a lot; sometimes it is minimal because the company selling to the OEM prefers to have all contacts be between the OEM's regular sales force and the customer, or even between a "dedicated" salesperson and the customer (dedicated because the customer needs someone who can understand its own complex product, and this requires a specialized salesperson who attends only to this particular customer).

Systems Integrators

In order to understand what a systems integrator does, let's consider a business situation based on an actual case. A high-tech company gets wind of what looks like a good international sales opportunity. The potential customer is the Ministry of Finance of Transbaltania. Transbaltanians do a lot of importing, and the citizens are tired of seeing underpaid customs agents driving Mercedes; the importers are tired of paying bribes and having to get eighteen signatures on a document to release a shipment of canned tomatoes; the docks are crammed with rotting cases whose contents are a mystery . . . you get the picture. The Ministry of Finance, which has responsibility for customs administration, has decided that one way to get things under control is to "computerize" customs operations. The estimated size of the hardware part of the deal (and that's what the high-tech company is interested in) is over $2 million. Best of all, though Transbaltania is fourth from the bottom on the list of the world's poorest countries, if the company wins this deal, it is certain to be paid, and not in kropecks, the local currency, but in dollars! The reason is that the entire deal is financed by the World Bank, and that's how this organization pays.

It is likely, though, that the company doesn't have a representative in Transbaltania, or indeed anywhere within 5,000 miles of there. Also, such bids usually require other specialized equipment that this particular high-tech vendor does not produce and that it is not in a position to acquire.

It's in large deals like these (and not just internationally, of course) that systems integrators come in. These companies are sales channels that bid on the overall project, working with a number of manufacturers, each of whom supplies only a piece of the total package. Because it's their business to know these things, systems integrators may have been acquiring knowledge about the project for months or even years before the bid documents hit the street, so they're better prepared to win it than any of the individual companies whose products they will integrate into the overall solution for the customer. Normally, dealing effectively with a systems integrator to win a large contract requires that the high-tech company set up an ad hoc working team; this team may have engineers, salespeople, and financial people on it. Such teams can be effectively organized and managed by nontechnical people. Because there is always a time constraint on putting the deal together, there is a premium attached to effectively "driving the process." Participation in such a team is a good way for the nontechnical person in channels management to acquire experience in winning large chunks of business, and this always gets the favorable attention of senior management.

VARs

The term *VAR* stands for value-added reseller. These are channels who buy a product—say a computer—add something to it, and resell the package to the end user. The difference from the OEM is usually said to be that when a VAR is involved, the computer is sold with the manufacturer's name still on it. And everyone can see that it's a computer.

What is it that the VAR adds? It can be a piece of specialized software that enables a specialized need to be met. Let's say that a VAR has developed some software that enables the chocolate manufacturing process to become more efficient by a factor of 10 percent by more accurately controlling the quantity of chocolate liquor squeezed from cacao nibs. Chocolate makers from Brussels, Belgium to Hershey, Pennsylvania are beating its door down. The VAR decides to sell a company's computers preloaded with its software. Yes, it's like an ISV, but it has inside contacts with a very specific industry segment and decides that it can sell a complete solution. This is a neat way for the computer manufacturer to sell into the chocolate industry. (The manufacturer's own sales force might all be chocoholics who would welcome the opportunity to acquire more personalized knowledge of the chocolate industry, but the manufacturer has determined that the market is bigger in, say, computerized sheep dipping, so it has them all attending a local ag extension course.)

VARs need a lot of support, as well as a system of tracking, because they are at a couple of removes from the manufacturing company—they buy from a distributor, who in turn buys from the company. The company has to set up a system to monitor their performance and keep track of how much business they are doing; channels management folks periodically carry out business reviews for this purpose. But it's just as important for the VARs to catch some of the spirit of the high-tech company they ultimately represent. Conferences, "kickoff meetings," technical and sales training sessions, and product launches are all means of helping to build a feeling of partnership. These sorts of events are partly business and partly like a reunion of an extended family, with considerable attention given to creating a personal, teamlike atmosphere. In this way channels management organizations try to bring about more contact between the manufacturer and the VAR without upsetting the primary VAR-distributor relationship. The requirements for this kind of work are an interest in business and an interest in people. It can be a lot of fun, and the nontechnical person can learn much about his or her own and customers' businesses.

Master Distributors

One of the worst things a high-tech manufacturer can have is inventory of unsold product on hand. It costs money, requires storage and insurance, and is demoralizing to think about. Having a distribution channel in place solves this and many other problems (although, as with anything in this life, there are tradeoffs). The master distributor purchases in large quantities, so the manufacturer gains efficiencies and predictability; the distributor then sells the product within a defined geographic area to resellers of various kinds, including VARs. The master distributor is usually required to provide the high-tech manufacturer with a "rolling forecast" of what it will sell over the next six months, so that the company can plan its parts requirements and better schedule its factories' operations.

To give you a picture of some of the problems that nontechnical people get involved with in managing distributors, consider first the ideal situation, which has never existed and will never exist, but which is still the dream of every channels manager. Ideally, the distributor's credit is superb, so there is no question that the company will get paid; it has a staff of well-trained salespeople who may sell directly to certain parts of the market, and who sell to resellers for the other parts. Because of the perfect mutual understanding that underlies the relationship between the high-tech manufacturer and the distributor, there is no danger that the manufacturer will find itself competing with its own distributor for a large chunk of business.

Distributors are limited by contract to certain geographical areas—*geos*, in high-tech lingo. In the ideal situation, the distributor's representative would rather deliver his first-born son personally to Pharaoh than ship even a cable outside its agreed territory of the western United States to, say, Tallahassee, or maybe Taipei.

Ideally, the master distributor is so happy with the deal the high-tech company has struck with it that it would never consider taking on a competitive line of equipment. Or if it were forced to do so by market circumstances, at least it would set up a distinct company to handle the competition's useless stuff. Finally, the distributor would be well funded and would insist on bearing its fair share of the costs of trade shows, advertising, and the like.

All of the problems that don't exist in the ideal situation do exist in real life, and they have to be managed. Managing distributors, like managing many other areas of business, calls for a delicate balance of toughness and diplomacy. The distributor is in a kind of partnership with the high-tech company, but whereas the distributor may (and almost always does) have many lines of products that it is carrying, the high-tech company has placed all or many of its eggs in the distributor's basket. If the relationship breaks down, it can be worse for the manufacturer, who may see its sales slump or even cease for a period of time in a given geo until a new distribution channel can be set up.

Many nontechnical people are found in channels management; it can be a most interesting and rewarding career area in the high-tech industry.

Marketing Communications

This area, known in the industry as *marcom*, was defined for me by the corporate director of marketing communications of a large high-tech hardware company:

> It essentially supports marketing objectives and business objectives. It includes advertising, press relations, trade shows, literature, sales promotion. And I think that with the advent of new technology, there'll be all kinds of multimedia that will fall into the same category as well.

It's unusual for people in marcom to have technical degrees. Often they come from the fine arts or journalism, but many educational backgrounds are represented in this area. Marcom people often feel that the high-tech culture, being centered so much on technology, tends to downgrade their function. One marcom specialist said:

> I think that frankly we have a lot more marketing knowledge than some of the "pure" marketing people. For example, we often find them claiming, 'Here is my marketing plan; we're going to go to these trade shows, we're going to do these advertisements,' and I'm going, 'That's not a marketing plan,

those are marcom tactics.' We are very much internal consultants to management right now. In our company, for example, few people understand the concept of branding. In a consumer company, the whole purpose is to establish a brand
and have brand loyalty. Most of our managers will not be able
to tell you what a brand is or its importance. Our [marcom]
people are strong functional experts with many years of experience.

The marketing communications function is a very important pillar
of support for the effort to move products from the high-tech company
to the customers. An example of this is trade shows. High tech, with its
rapidly changing and developing technology, depends to an unusual
degree on trade shows, of which there are many during the course of a
year. Just selecting which shows to be in and which ones to let go by is
an important decision. Having a presence at a trade show costs money—
for rental of space for a booth, construction or rental of the booth itself,
staffing and transportation, and design and printing of special promotional literature, videos, and other media. Budgets are limited, so it's
essential, once the decision to participate is made, that everything proceed smoothly. Organizing for such an event starts many months in
advance, and a high-tech company is usually in different stages of planning for a number of events at one time. All this takes a high degree of
brains and energy to bring off successfully, and the marcom function
has the prime responsibility for making it happen.

Press relations is another very sensitive area under the aegis of the
marcom department. What is said about a high-tech company in the
press can have an immediate effect on customers' decisions to buy or
not, the company's stock price, and the morale of its employees. The
marcom people handling PR have to have good judgment and know how
to deal with the media, and they must also have fast access to all levels
of management in the company.

Product literature isn't as sensitive as a press release, but in the
high-tech industry it's an extremely important adjunct to the selling
process. Brochures, catalogs, and "spec sheets" (glossy sheets of paper,
often with color photographs or drawings, giving the basic specifications
of the product) are very expensive to produce. Marcom has the task of
working with the product managers and business managers to determine when a product will "FCS" (first customer ship); the literature (or
"collateral material," in high-tech jargon) has to be planned and coor-
dinated accordingly.

So regardless of what the techies may think, marketing communications is an important function, and one that welcomes nontechnical people.

Operations

Operations is a general term for a group or department that is responsible for supplier management, materials procurement, and distribution of the products. Thus it watches the supply line going into the manufacturing plant and the distribution of the finished product to the shipping department. In some companies, forecasting of orders and shipments is located in this department. Different enterprises may organize these functions in different ways, but they all exist somewhere in the high-tech company.

Supplier management means assuring that the suppliers of raw materials—or, in the case of the high tech industry, components—understand the company's requirements as regards delivery times, cost, and specifications of the materials. Distribution involves the maintenance of sufficient stocks in a warehouse to meet forecasted needs and the physical fulfillment of orders. Materials management, or procurement, involves taking the sales forecast, comparing it to existing stocks, and placing a purchase order with suppliers to make up the difference. After a while materials managers get adept at reading forecasts and building in safety factors; there's nothing as agonizing as having a huge backlog of orders that can't be shipped because the materials to make the products weren't ordered in time. The deputy operations manager of a software company told me:

> You have to use your judgment—am I usually high? Low? Then, on top of that, you have to concern yourself with pricing models, especially in the software print world. If you buy small quantities, you pay high prices; if you buy a lot, the prices drop way down. You have to balance the risk of obsolesence with the unit cost considerations.

High-tech companies are moving to "outsource" the distribution elements of the function. Forecasting, supplier management, and materials management, however, will almost certainly remain inside the company; they are too sensitive and too critical to entrust to an outside contractor. As the deputy operations manager told me:

> We sat around a table and decided what we wanted to keep in-house. The actual picking up of boxes is what we're getting

rid of. We'll tell the outside company how many boxes of [product] to stock, and then the order will come in, it will get transferred electronically to the distribution company, and they will pull it off the shelf. When they run out of material, they'll call us up and tell us they need more.

The operations department of a high-tech company tends to be fairly stable, and so new employment opportunities don't open up often in the more mature companies. Younger companies are a different matter, however. Since operations is not a glamorous field, a lot of the hiring is done through networking. If you learn of an entry-level opportunity in this field or if you have some special experience that would qualify you for a midlevel position, you can try for it without fearing that the lack of a technical background will keep you out of the running. What is important for operations positions is familiarity with math, having an orderly mind, and being able to deal with multiple projects at once. The educational background of the deputy operations manager cited above was literature and economics. He also has an MBA. One person reporting to him has an undergraduate degree in literature.

Typically operations is a tough area to get out of, so far as moving into sales or marketing. Product management and finance, however, are areas into which operations people have moved.

Order Operations

Order ops, as it is usually called, involves assuring that orders are "clean" when they are put into the system. This means that the part numbers match the written description of the product, that financial terms are met (letters of credit, net thirty days, and so forth), and that there's nothing about the order that would cause it to get held up. If the order is international, an order ops person will ensure that all export licenses are in order. Order ops people deal with the factory or operations groups to know when orders are likely to ship; they will inform sales reps if a delay is anticipated. They know how long, for example, it takes to build a certain type of computer; if there is a shortage looming, the order ops staff will try to set some priorities to ensure that the most time-sensitive orders are filled first. This often calls for reserves of patience and diplomacy.

Order ops is another function that is not glamorous. But it does have the advantages of being nontechnical and of affording those who work in it the chance to learn a lot about the innards of a fast-paced business. And you needn't have a technical degree or a business degree.

At one of the hardware companies in Silicon Valley, there's a young woman working in international order operations. She has a degree in art history—just like the woman I mentioned in the Introduction. Starting as a receptionist, she became an admin after a year, and a year after that she entered order ops. She told me:

> When I was an admin, I really didn't know anything about the products. Now I know all the desktops, desksides, peripherals, software. So I really think I've picked up a lot working here. And you have to know it in order to answer questions from customers, and sometimes from the salespeople as well.

From her present position, it would be possible to go in any of several different directions, including finance, operations, and even sales.

Product Marketing

Product marketing, sometimes also called product management, is a very important job in the high-tech industry. It's usually the sort of position you work up to, although in a smaller company or for a product that management considers ancillary to the main product line you might be able to move into it more easily. Product marketing managers are responsible for learning the market's requirements for a product, overseeing all aspects of production and introduction of the product to the markets, forecasting initial and ongoing sales, and then sticking with the product until its EOL. It's sort of like being a geneticist, obstetrician, pediatrician, internist, gerontologist, and undertaker, only these roles occur within a period of eighteen months to four years instead of a human lifetime. Product marketing managers work closely with other kinds of marketing people as well as with the sales force and the engineers who actually design the product.

Product marketing is primarily a function that links the prospective *users* of a product to the *designers* of the product in such a fashion as to make the product more useful, efficient, or cost-effective. A person working in this field takes responsibility for seeing that this is done for one or more products—sometimes a complete line of products, such as computer monitors or printers. The purpose of this function is to make sure that the company does not end up designing and building products that are a delight to the engineers who designed them, but that no one will want to buy as was the case with the instrument company mentioned earlier in this chapter. The product marketer will work closely with the design engineers on the one hand and with the potential customers on the other, while also taking into consideration the special requirements of the production and service people. If everything works out, the final products will be useful, easy to build and service, and priced competitively, and hence will sell well in the market.

Because they work so closely with highly technical engineers, most product marketing folks have acquired a good command of the technology. Companies like to see people who are engineers or who have MBAs, or ideally both, in such positions. But many have no technical training other than what they've picked up along the way. I can think offhand of three successful product marketing managers whose formal education was, respectively, in political science, biology, and history.

So you really can't say the gates are closed. It's like so much in the high-tech world—if you want it, you can make it happen.

One interesting thing product managers get to do is have direct contact with customers. This is perhaps their greatest utility to the high-tech company. The sales force is interested in selling; the product manager is interested in selling something the customer *needs*, and he or she is in a position to do something if the customer looks confused, or aghast, when a new product concept is presented. This is not to malign the sales force; obviously it *prefers* to sell what the customer wants, but it *must* sell whatever is on the price list. The product marketing managers make sure the products on the price list make sense.

President

The president of a high-tech company works for the shareholders, as represented by the board of directors, and though it is unlikely that you will start your career in high tech at this level, you ought to be aware that having a high-tech background isn't required for the job, or for many other top management positions, such as vice-president of sales, marketing, or finance. Scott McNealy, president and CEO of Sun Microsystems, majored in economics, and then went on to business school. After that he worked in the automobile industry for a couple of years in sales and manufacturing roles. He used his manufacturing knowledge in his first high-tech job with a small startup company. He says:

> I basically stumbled my way around. . . . I said, "Would you give me a plant tour?" And [the manufacturing manager] said sure. . . . I went, "Wow, what are all these little black things?" He said, "Those are DRAM." I said, "What do they do?" and

he said, "They control the operating system." I said, "What does the operating system do?"

It's unlikely at that point that anyone would have bet on McNealy's chances of eventually running one of the most successful high-tech companies in the world. He set out to learn as much as possible from others.

> The first thing I did was I went and cozied up to a hardware engineer and a software engineer, and I said, "I've got to learn this stuff." . . . It would be about six or seven o'clock at night when they were still there. I would go into their offices and they would give me a chalk talk, and I would say, "Start from the basics and just teach me." . . . The other thing I did was to go down to Mission College and I enrolled in basic electronics classes. . . . I learned volts, amps, all the rest of that. I knew nothing. . . . it was quite an experience. It was a lot of hard work, but I got to the point where I could work a voltmeter, and I'd go out on the [factory] floor . . . and they'd go, "Wow!" They were blown away that I was actually making progress. The fact that I cared and I wanted to learn made it a lot easier for people to deal with my ignorance. . . .
>
> Today I'm still not sure I understand how those electrons move around on those little chips, but I have a pretty good feel for design cycles, life cycles, where the technology is at the state of the art, and where invention happens, how it happens. And what kind of people you need to get on board, what kind of environment you need to set up. I don't need to do the invention, I just need to set up the environment that facilitates the invention, and away we go!

In case you think it could never happen to you, perhaps you're right—it won't just *happen*, but you can *make* it happen. Get some experience, and after a few years, if you're bold and willing to take a chance (there was no guarantee that Sun Microsystems would survive its first five years), get involved with a startup, say as vice-president of marketing. See Chapter 7, "Startups."

Sales

It's absolutely amazing to discover where high-tech salespeople come from. They can have undergraduate majors in psychology, history, economics, literature, and many other nontechnical fields. There seems to be no logical connection whatsoever between the formal education these people have had and their present jobs. It's a field that lends itself naturally to people who are gregarious and confident. That being the case, there's no reason you too can't edge yourself into a sales position. It takes some time, because you do have to have a fairly thorough understanding of your product to be successful, and you have to sell a sales manager on your ability to acquire such an understanding in order to get the job in the first place. But selling yourself as a sales type of person is far more important than product knowledge, which can be acquired fairly easily. The two most important prerequisites for a high-tech sales job are being able to communicate effectively with different sorts of people and a strong desire to make a lot of money. The least important is having high-tech educational credentials. In addition, though, you have to be interested in business. As Scott McNealy of Sun Microsystems says:

> Most of selling is not a technical problem, most of it is a business problem. I think people really get confused and aimed the wrong way in thinking that you've got to be able to speak the bits and bytes.

A software salesman told me of his nontechnical background:

> I started in English and philosophy, and after a year of fifteenth-century poets and even more abstract philosophy, I figured that wasn't what I wanted to do. So I moved into psychology and finished up with a B.S. in psychology. I got a graduate research assistant slot and started out for the Ph.D. But I realized after a year and a half that I didn't want to do that either. I got my M.A. so I'd have something to show for my effort. And I also got a second M.A. in broadcasting. It was easy to do because many of the credits were the same. I started in that field with a student internship, but after three months they started paying me so that I'd keep regular hours. And then I moved to a TV station and worked there for two and a half years.

Not terribly high-tech so far, is it? But he's now making about $120,000 a year in high-tech sales. That doesn't include some special bonuses, or the trip to a fancy resort with his wife when he makes his yearly sales quota. How did he do it? He started by writing freelance articles for a PC magazine while working for the TV station, and got interested in computer technology. He bought a PC and wrote some more articles. Then he got a job in public relations in a large hardware company. Then he talked a sales manager into giving him a chance to prove he could sell. Because he could communicate effectively, he was (and is) an effective salesman.

High-tech salespeople who are good (and there is no other kind, because the bad ones leave quickly) are the princes and princesses of the industry. A youthful hardware salesman who (he might be in his twenties) had no doubts about that:

> Let me tell you something. I'm making my numbers and exceeding them every quarter. No one—*no one*—can get between me and my customers. I can tell the sales manager to f_____ h_____ and he'll do it, because I'm making him successful. Not even the president of this company can get in my way. If he does, I'm out of here like a flash!

Yes, there's a little bit of ego there all right. Yet deservedly so. Salespeople are out on the thin edge. If it weren't for them, the business would stop. The relationships they have with their customers are their really precious stock in trade, and there are moments when they feel that no one at home is supporting them, that they are carrying the weight of the entire enterprise on their shoulders. Prices are revised and no one told them. Products are EOL'd and no one told them.

Sales representatives are seldom found in the office; they are usually out calling on customers (who could be end users of the products or one of the sales channels). When they are in the office, they may be following up to be sure that the orders they put into the system have been filled and shipped. Generally sales reps are not credited with a sale until the product has actually been shipped to the customer, and toward the end of the quarter (high-tech salespeople have quarterly goals) they

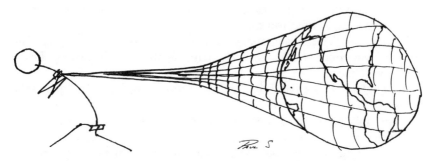

What the high-tech salesperson really wants.

may spend a good deal of time in the office on the phone, trying to iron out any problems that may prevent shipment. These can include credit issues, competition with other salespeople for a limited supply of a product, or sometimes simply a misplaced or lost order.

Sales reps are expected to be very familiar with the products they sell, but this does not mean a deep technical knowledge of how they are constructed. They read up on new products and consult with product managers to find out what the new products will do and when the expected FCS (first customer shipment) date will be. High-tech sales is a tense, exciting (sometimes nervewracking), and very well paid occupation.

When you live like that, you love the people that support you and you hate the people that get in your way. Which brings us to another category of jobs.

Sales Support

The sales support function takes many forms in the high-tech industry, but the idea is the same: Make the system work so that the sales reps can do their job and make their numbers, and everybody can get paid next week. It's an important position because it takes care of everything concerning the customer that the salesperson does not have time to do. And that's a lot. Salespeople, after all, live or die by their numbers, which are calculated every quarter by merciless number crunchers located in a basement office. If the salesperson misses his or her number by a small amount, maybe the quota was set a bit too high, or maybe a customer decided to defer half the order until the next quarter, but it's a sure thing then. If the salesperson misses the number by a very large amount, clearly this was due to some uncontrollable act of God—a seismic event, perhaps, or a collapse of the Nikkei stock average. Or perhaps the customer's treasurer ran off with the bank account, the customer is now bankrupt, and thus a major sale on which the rep had been working for months simply fell through.

No matter. The sales manager develops a steely look in his eye. The number crunchers send their statements upstairs. The moving finger writes, and having writ, moves on. *Mene, mene, tekel, upharsin.* Thou hast been weighed in the balances, and art found wanting. One quarter is excusable. Two quarters aren't.

The only sure friend the sales rep has is the sales support person. While the rep is off chasing more business, the sales support person may be finding out what happened to an order the customer swore was faxed in last Tuesday or alerting the rep to a problem with the credit people. He's the person the customers can call when the rep is on the road; they know he'll find the answer, and get things done. The sales support people may visit customers with the sales rep from time to time, or they may work entirely behind the scenes. They can ensure that the customer got the literature, the price book, the promotional stuff that the marketing people developed. They do everything in their power to assist the sales reps to make their numbers, and as the quarter draws to a close, they become the reps' alter egos. These people get as close to the customer as one can get without being in sales. They don't make as much money, but they're well paid. And they don't have a sales quota to make every quarter, which means they sleep reasonably well the nights preceding the solstices and equinoxes. It's nice work.

Technical Writing and Editing

The high-tech industry desperately needs qualified writers to prepare all sorts of technical manuals and publications. Though there has been some improvement in recent years as good writers have become aware of the need, the quality of much of the (very extensive) literature that pervades the industry is poor. Recently some colleges and junior colleges have begun offering courses in technical writing. You should realize that companies usually charge for the documentation that accompanies their products, and that this documentation can range from a simple folded piece of paper to many thousands of pages. (Currently much documentation is being transferred to compact disks that will display contents on a computer screen.) Since customers rely on the manuals to get their systems to work, and since they often pay extra for this material, there is a considerable push to improve its quality. Documentation is one of the most critical products a high-tech company provides; in fact, it not only helps the user understand and work with the product, it also serves the high-tech manufacturer as marketing and product positioning material. So writing positions are of great importance to the sales organization in the high-tech company, and technical writers are treated with respect and well paid.

The technical writer usually works as a full member of a team that is developing a new product (or some part of one) or working to improve an existing product, so he or she gets the raw information firsthand from the technical, service, and marketing people on the team. Writers tend to become quite expert in the areas of technology they work on. Most do not come from a technical background, but rather have degrees in literature or some other area of the humanities.

Because the writer is a team member, he or she may acquire a biased view of the relative importance of the project. That's where the technical editor comes in. The technical editor not only performs normal editing functions, but also can provide perspective, consistency, and continuity. Individual project teams are formed and dissolve as their missions are accomplished, or sometimes abandoned. The editor can make sure that every bit of information is incorporated into the final document in a manner that both is internally coherent, and matches with what the company has said elsewhere. As an editor said to me:

> As the editor for the software development framework pro-ject, when I get a submission [of material], I go through and make sure that what is said is consistent with, and not out of proportion to, things we've said about similar topics else-where. And I get edited as well; we have an outside contractor that looks at what I do. In an important project like this, there are a number of levels [of control]. We issue a document of about five hundred pages every six months. If anything is out of sync, it can cause major problems.

Another ex-teacher has an undergraduate degree in English, and a master's in teaching, both from the University of California at Berkeley.

> I taught junior high and high school for eleven years. At the end of those eleven years, education was starting its grand decline in California. Money was drying up. Class sizes were getting larger. I was thirty-five years old. I had applied for other positions in the school district that would have been promotions for me, and had not gotten them. I just felt that my options were really narrow.

> So I got to feeling kind of depressed, actually. So I got a sum-mer job at [company] doing technical editing and writing. I had never done that before. I met one of the engineers that worked there on a Sierra Club hike, and he gave me an intro-duction to some of the people there.

This woman went on to describe the change from the public school environment in these words:

> I was very relaxed! I didn't have all the stresses and strains of classroom teaching and grading papers, teaching writing. On the job I could get everything done really fast. All the people in my department were amazed. And I was amazed that they were amazed!

Telesales

"Telesales? Ugh!" I heard you say it. But this type of work in high tech is a little different from its civilian counterpart. Instead of pushing cosmetics or exercise equipment on people who would rather enjoy their dinner than talk to you, telesales involves calling the attention of potential customers to products or services that can save them money by making their businesses more efficient. The initial reaction of the people you call is to *listen* to you, not to hang up. They actually *want* to hear from you. This in itself is a wonderful thing, but better still is that after a while you will have mastered every aspect of the product you're selling through fielding the questions people throw at you. And you start to learn about your customers' businesses as well—their names, what they do, where they are located, and so forth. In other words, you start to get immersed in the high-tech world outside your company through the end users of whatever it is you're selling. If you're calling the MIS manager at a large financial institution, you will start to learn about that field and feel comfortable dealing with it. If you're dealing with the medical industry, you start to get immersed in its particular concerns. More important still, you add this experience to your resumé; you have been on the front line dealing with customers. This is the sort of thing that impresses hiring managers greatly.

Training

Many nontechnical people get their start in the high-tech industry through training. Some companies offer lists of courses that would put a small college to shame. Different from customer training, these courses are aimed at employees of the company; they can cover everything from how to put on an effective presentation, to negotiating with the Japanese, to time management, to computer systems administration. Other companies offer some in-house courses and contract outside for others. Some of these courses provide skills needed to do your job better and some are highly technical, aimed at providing specific knowledge in a new technical area.

This emphasis on short-term, highly specific training reflects a belief on the part of the top management of the company that colleges and universities simply cannot keep up with the rapid pace of technological change. In the words of a senior manager:

> Technical education has become vocational education. Would you go to school for four years to learn how to turn out cranks for automobiles?

Nor can they provide other kinds of training of the quality and in the concentration that business wants. If you're going to be dealing with the Japanese next month, the company wants you to get inside the basic do's and don'ts in a couple of days, not a couple of semesters.

All this training has to be planned, developed, and delivered. Nontechnical people coming from the world of education may feel more comfortable in this environment than in others, at least initially. A woman who teaches at a large corporation said:

> I had a bachelor's degree in social services. Then I went into retailing for a year and a half before going to a telecommunications company as a specialist hooking up phone lines. I was there for about six and a half years. There was no formal training there, just an older person I worked with. But I kept getting promoted, from specialist to senior specialist to supervisor. Finally I ended up as a manager. But I didn't get technical, because I was more on the people side. The company had no money for training, so they asked for volunteers to train others, and my department was going along well, so I volunteered. The training was in how to supervise. I went from that job into high tech, as a training specialist.
>
> Training is a big field now in high tech, and it's more secure than it was ten years ago. Even Bill Clinton has recognized this.

There are several nice things about being in the training field in high tech. People generally show up for class on time, they don't throw spitballs, and they are motivated. There's no board of education, and there are no angry parents to deal with. Also, the pay tends to be good. People who have labored in the public education field for years tend to appreciate these differences. As one of them told me:

> I worked twelve years for the [state] educational system. Not as a teacher, as an administrator. When I came out here, I decided I wanted to make the move from the public sector to the private sector in spades. My perception was that the public sector is kind of looked down on, like a forty-seventh cousin. People who work in it are not generally regarded as professionals. So I decided I'd show 'em!
>
> I had a horrible feeling that I wasn't qualified for anything. People talked to me about going into training because I had an education background. That was also my undergraduate

degree. I ended up going into a software development training program. I didn't teach in it, I managed the program. I remember the first visit I took with my boss to meet with a bunch of engineers. He told me not to talk to anybody. He didn't want them to know I didn't know anything!

The woman who made the above remarks has now been in a computer company for some eight years and has a very senior position. She works hard, drives a new sports car, and is dreaming about buying a yacht and singlehanding it to Hawaii, for openers.

3

The Successful Job Hunt

There is no one sure-fire method for getting a job in the high-tech industry. If there were, the secret would have leaked out by now and you wouldn't be reading this book; you'd be working away in whatever high-tech company you chose. And the reason that there isn't a single golden key to the high-tech door is found in the many variables that reflect your uniqueness as a human being and the complexity of the high-tech industry. Some of these variables you have little or no control over, such as the ever-changing human needs of the high-tech industry, your educational background, the length and type of work experience you've had, competition for any given position, and the ups and downs of the economy.

If you do not have control over the above variables, you *can* have complete control over how you plan, organize, and carry out your high-tech job hunt. And you *must* attain this control and maintain it throughout the process if you are to be successful. Most of us, when we are job hunting, bring to this task varying amounts of logic and emotion. If you've just been laid off, for example, you may be full of emotion—anger at your former employer, fear of the future, self-doubt, and so forth. If you've been unemployed for several weeks or months, you may be depressed and have feelings of shame or guilt or bitterness. These emotions shouldn't be buried or suppressed; on the contrary, they should be brought out and dealt with, by therapy if necessary. But they must not be allowed to influence your high-tech job search. They drain energy and stifle motivation. And they can get in the way of your constantly improving your hunting skills. So take whatever steps are required to get rid of unproductive and harmful feelings.

On the other hand, if you've been working at a job for several years and just decide that it's time for a move to high tech, you probably do not have as much emotional baggage to deal with. This will make it easier for you to plan a campaign.

You *can* get a job in the high-tech industry if you go about it with intelligence, determination, and *persistence.* As a Shakespeare scholar working in a software company told me:

> Persistence is what counts. If you want to do something, never give up! Under any circumstances! If you want to do it, it will happen. Most people give up remarkably easily. They've got too much of their own ego in it.

Your Self-Tailored Plan

What you must do to get inside the walls of the high-tech industry is to develop you *own* plan that will express your own uniqueness, and then execute it. Most plans benefit by being written down, and your plan for your job hunt is no exception. What should go into such a plan?

There are five steps to a high-tech job campaign plan. They are:

1. Self-appraisal and attitude adjustment
2. Background acquisition
3. Identification of opportunities
4. Résumés
5. Interviews

When you write your plan, what you're really doing is setting up a record-keeping system. You must keep a written record of your opportunities and who your contacts are for each one, a copy of the résumé sent to each person, and a few lines on each interview you have—with whom, when, additional names for your network (to be discussed later), and phone/fax numbers. Writing down the record of your job hunt will discipline you, and discipline is what you need to be successful.

Self-Appraisal

Your personal plan starts with as objective as possible an appraisal of the kind of person you are. You have to know yourself, and whether you feel you'd fit into the environment of the high-tech industry.

There are several tests that, properly administered and interpreted, can tell you a lot about yourself and how you'd fit into the environment of the high-tech industry. These tests are administered by employment and career counselors and psychologists, and are worth investigating. The four that are usually at the top of any career counselor's list are these; of course, the tests mentioned here are designed to be given and interpreted by professionals. I suggest that you discuss them with a career counselor who can explain each to you, along with its potential meaning for your own career decisions.

1. *California Psychological Inventory (CPI)*. This is a test that was developed in the early 1960s; it predicts performance in social settings, school, and job functions. It is very well known. The test has eighteen different scales on which behavior is measured, and it is easy to relate these to work life. The score for a particular scale might indicate that the person taking the test likes to work in settings where the job is tightly defined and there are clear milestones for measuring progress. This is usually not the case in the high-tech industry.

2. *Campbell Interest and Skill Survey™ (CISS™).** This test measures both your interest in various occupations and your self-reported skills. This inclusion of the skills component is one of the strengths of this test; the subject might have strong interest in being a world-renowned restaurateur, but the interest alone will not carry him very far if he lacks some of the skills required by this occupation. On the other hand, the test can indicate occupational areas where he may have both a high level of interest and high skill levels; these might offer much more rewarding careers.

3. *The Sixteen Personality Factor Questionnaire (16PF)*. This test was constructed by examining most of the adjectives by which personal behavior is defined and reducing them to a set of sixteen bipolar characteristics that underlie them. Some of these include: Reserved/Outgoing, Trusting/Suspicious, Practical/Imaginative, and Group-Dependent/Self-Sufficient.

4. *The Myers-Briggs Type Indicator*. This is a very well known self-administered test of personality and preferences. It has been used for many years in career counseling.

Chapter 5 deals with culture and makes the points that different cultures are found in different high-tech companies and that you should feel comfortable being in the culture. But on the larger front, you need to ask yourself how happy you would be in an industry where the work is characterized by the following:

- Little direction from superiors
- Long hours
- Work judged by peers
- High pay

*CISS and Campbell Interest and Skill Survey are trademarks owned by David Campbell, Ph.D.

- Fast pace
- Responsibility for own career development
- Speaking before groups
- Pushiness valued
- Multicultural, multiethnic
- Performance valued rather than style
- Most employees are young
- Too little time to do the work
- Frequent retraining/reeducation necessary
- Must deal with technical people
- Constant reorganization
- Use of jargon
- Deal with uncertainty

Career counselors, using the tests mentioned above, can help you with these issues. People do grow and adjust to new environments, so I don't think that you'll reach the conclusion that you *shouldn't* proceed with your high-tech job search, at least to the point of seeing firsthand what is available for you out there. But you ought to start out with your eyes open.

Once you've concluded that you do want to proceed with your high-tech job quest, you should do a little attitudinal work. A job hunt can be frustrating. It might help at the beginning to reframe it and say that it's really a process of making friends with lots of interesting people. Here and there along the way job possibilities start to appear, and sooner or later along comes the right one. This has happened to many people I've met who are now working as professionals in the high-tech industry. These people came from the following fields and educational backgrounds, among others: teaching (elementary, junior high, high school, college, music, art), educational administration, television and newspaper journalism, urban planning, psychology, secretarial, theology, machine tool operation, sports broadcasting. They wanted to get in, and they made it happen. A young woman told me:

> Initially I was turned down for the position. There were two hundred people applying for two positions. I didn't get it the first round. But then the husband of the person who had got it got transferred, so they called me back a month later for a second round [of interviews]. It was difficult because there were a lot of qualified people applying for it. For example, one of the people had six years of experience in the telecommunications field. I had zero experience. I think mostly they hired me because they liked me.

There's that persistence again! Determine that you're going to make moving into the high-tech industry a real campaign, and one that will involved a lot of learning and growing just by itself. You may luck out and get your perfect job in a week—it has happened. More likely it will take three to six months to get inside the walls of the industry.

The industry uses the term *mindset* a lot. It means having the right attitude and locking it in the way a navigator sets a radio compass course on an airplane. The plane flies through storm clouds and high winds, but it's locked on course and gets to its destination. You've got to do the same thing.

You ought also to set your expectations for your first high-tech job realistically. If there was agreement among the persons interviewed for this book on any single point, it was that the important thing in looking for a job in the high-tech industry was just to get inside the walls. Once inside, in any position at all, you can maneuver to get the position you really want and deserve. A channels marketing person reports that:

> My cousin got in by being a janitor! Then he moved on from there. Get in any way you can; there's no one way to do it.

It's really important for you to keep this in mind. Once inside the walls of the high-tech industry, your feet off the battlements and firmly on solid ground, you can start wielding all those formidable weapons you've brought with you concealed about your person. But when you are still on the outside, in the eyes of those already in the high-tech industry, you inevitably bear the burden of proving that you really belong. The high-tech industry offers vastly greater opportunities to expand your existing job, or move to a new one, than any other field. So an important thing is not to get hung up at the beginning on status or salary or job title. A woman who came from a nontechnical job into a telesales support position for a high-tech component distributor told me:

> One of the things that got them to hire me in the first place was that I was inexperienced, so they didn't have to pay me as much as anyone else. But I was willing to take that step because I was able to learn some new skills.

And another stated:

> If somebody really wants to get into the technical field, I'd say take whatever position you could, just to learn. Sacrifice a

couple of years of low salary to get the experience. Then take
that experience somewhere else.

Your task is to become one of "them," that is, an insider. Most of us
who have been working in a given field for a few years, even if we feel
that our labors have been undervalued and, especially, underpaid and
our natural talents largely ignored, still have acquired some stature and
a respectable self-image. It is natural for us to expect that this should be
recognized by the high-tech industry. Sometimes during the job interview process this feeling gets in the way, because we sense that our
background isn't getting the full respect it deserves.

To understand why this occurs, you'll have to appreciate what is
going through the minds of the interviewers, particularly the human
resources people and the hiring manager. The HR people who get involved in hiring are terribly process-oriented, particularly in the larger
companies. Their task is to winnow through a huge pile of résumés and
produce five to ten for each position, which they present to the hiring
manager for consideration. Of course they want to produce some really
good candidates for the position, but in the day-to-day hurly-burly of
their work, they see their job as *getting rid of* large numbers of applicants.
Just the fact that you come from outside the industry may furnish them
with that distinguishing characteristic that enables them to cast aside
your résumé in good conscience. If you are fortunate enough to make it
to the stage of getting a call from HR for a screening interview, you must
at all costs avoid giving the caller the idea that you think you're really
doing the company a favor by applying for this position, as it's less important and prestigious that the one you currently have, or used to have.
Never come across as being casual about applying for a position. A
young man I know was trying to switch jobs from a software company
into a networking company. Not being experienced in interviewing, he
thought he should come across as "cool," and so he told the HR person
that this was one of a number of opportunities he was looking at.
Though he was one of three candidates that had reached this stage, his
remarks sunk him; the HR person later reported to the headhunter that
had referred him:

> I thought we were just one of a bunch of opportunities he was
> looking at. I wasn't sure of his commitment, and I didn't want
> to run the risk he might leave us after a few weeks.

It's generally wise to avoid the HR department for as long as possible during the hiring process. Sending them your résumé, particularly
when times are tough for job seekers, is like hoping to win the lottery.

If you can get before the hiring manager directly, you've got a giant leg up on other candidates. We'll be considering this later in the chapter, but for now you should consider the hiring manager's state of mind, and how your attitude toward the job opportunity might affect it for better or for worse. No hiring manager really enjoys the hiring process, because he or she doesn't get "goaled" or measured on it, yet it takes up a lot of time. In the high-tech industry, few hiring managers really trust the judgment of the HR people, but they figure that they certainly don't want to plough through hundreds of résumés themselves. When you are facing the hiring manager and you come across as really interested in and committed to the position, and don't raise a lot of questions that smack of "is this all there is?" or "where can I expect to move to in a year?" you make the manager feel that the time he or she spent with you was really worthwhile—you're genuinely a good candidate.

So it'll help you to be willing to start with whatever you can get, give it your best, and move when the time is ripe. Here's a comment from a man who came to high tech with a couple of years' work experience in a financial institution:

> [The first job] was kind of doing everything including carrying the kitchen sink around. This was in manufacturing. I was an expediter, so I would run around from the factory to shipping to order processing. I was just making a bunch of connections. It wasn't something I wanted to do. But it paid well and got me an opportunity to find out what was going on.

And from a young woman channels manager:

> Over here they would give almost anyone a chance. Once you get your foot in the door, that's all it takes; you're able to do what you want after that.

Another important part of your attitude as you start out has to do with confidence. Unlike many other work environments, high-tech companies and managers respect people who are a little pushy. Once you're inside, the term is "aggressive," and you will never lose points for having too much of this quality. While you're still an outsider, however, you have to tone it down a little bit, though not much. A woman who has been in the industry about five years, and who has counseled her friends on getting high-tech jobs, observed:

> People need to be pretty aggressive to get in. Just sending résumés over the fax just doesn't cut it. You can be pretty

aggressive and not be obnoxious; just get a little more in people's face and market yourself appropriately. [Job seekers] always seem to approach it by sending letters or E-mails and leaving messages. I don't know too much about it, but I definitely know that's not the way to get a job.

Certainly if you approach your job search scared to death because you're going to get involved with technology, it'll show. Take the word of a reporter and writer who became a top salesman in a software company:

I went down to the local computer store. They were offering a full-day course. They sat you down at a PC and taught you the beginnings of BASIC, which I've never used since, but at least they gave me the minimal confidence that I didn't have to be scared of bits and bytes.

To sum up, once your self-appraisal leads you to believe that the high-tech industry and you could get along pretty well, you should:

• Treat the job hunt as an enjoyable exploration of a new area.
• Set your expectations realistically as regards job type and level.
• Be persistent and never give up.
• Be confident in the face of technology.

Background Acquisition

Whether and to what degree this is necessary depends on your education, your work experience, and the nature of the position you're after. These days it's difficult to get a job in the high-tech industry if you have absolutely no familiarity at all with the technology. That's so even if in your field there would seem to be no necessity for knowing technology—say, public relations. The problem is that your résumé will be devoid of any of the buzzwords that count in the industry. So you will tend to lose out to another person who may not be as well qualified as you for the actual job, but whose application makes him or her seem to be an insider. And whereas a good résumé won't assure you of getting a job, it's a certainty that a bad one will knock you out of the running. One of the characteristics of good résumé is that it tells the reader instantly whether or not there's a likely fit between you and your potential high-tech workgroup. If there's no reference to technology, the inference may be drawn, however unfairly, that there isn't a fit.

Another problem is that if you haven't had any exposure to technology, you may not come across to hiring managers as being confident that you can do the job. In fact, if you've sealed yourself off from computers and software up until now, chances are you really do lack confidence that you can survive in the high-tech world. Since there is in fact nothing particularly difficult about the technology at the level you'll need to master it, you may as well bite the bullet and tackle this psychological challenge by doing as the reporter mentioned above did: Get some direct exposure to the technology as part of your job hunt. How do you do this?

First, get a computer if you do not have one already! If you don't have a lot of money, get a used 386 PC or Macintosh; they're really cheap. But be sure to get one with full documentation. Read the hardware documentation. Try to master it. Get a computer glossary; either buy one at a bookstore or use the library's. Try to understand every term. Take your computer's cover off (be sure it's unplugged) and identify the components. If you can't identify them, ask a friend to help you.* Then join a users' group. Go to every meeting (these are also good job networking places). Your local hardware or software dealer should be able to give you information on where and when the next meeting will be held. Members of users' groups like to give advice. Remember that a lot of coming across as a high-tech person is nothing more nor less than being able to use technical terms and jargon. Hanging around users' groups, you won't be able to avoid picking up the specialized language of the industry.

Most high-tech job seekers today can truthfully claim *some* familiarity with some kind of computer because of the proliferation of PCs and Macs in the school systems. Few nontechnical persons, however, can speak knowledgeably about what makes up a computer, what its operating system does, how it communicates with a printer or disk drive, and the functions of its central processing unit and memory. Being able to do this will give you confidence and will place you a notch or two above the competition.

Then arrange to take a course or two. They're given everywhere—at adult education centers, colleges and junior colleges, career centers, and so forth. Which courses? Courses that are basic, but that take you *beyond your own PC and its manuals.* You want to learn about the basic electronics involved in computing, about operating systems and what they do, about networks and what they do. Looking at a catalog of courses and course descriptions in the high-tech field can be very frustrating because there are so many, and because the descriptions won't

*An excellent book, notable for its textual clarity and fine illustrations, is *How Computers Work* by Ron White (Emeryville, Calif.: Ziff-Davis Press, 1993).

mean much to you at this stage. Choosing a course from a catalog description alone is a roll of the dice. Before you sign up for a course, contact the teacher (who is often associated in some way with the industry—another good networking contact!). Teachers love to give advice even more than the rest of us do, and if you can get a good half hour with one, he or she can give you invaluable advice on which courses to take given your background and those areas where there are the most hiring opportunities. (By the way, if you are planning to stay in the area, you should get in contact with your teachers every so often. They rarely get this kind of attention and will reciprocate by keeping you in mind for any job opportunity they hear about.)

If you've never done any acting or public speaking, consider taking a one- or two-day course in interviewing skills. It is absolutely essential that you be able to come across in an interview as organized, calm, collected, and thoughtful, having a sense of humor, and being able to *listen*. Many people have good backgrounds but shoot themselves in the foot during the interview process, and so never get the chance to show how well they can do in the position. Being able to present ideas effectively is one of the most important skill requirements of nontechnical people in the high-tech industry; the hiring interview is the first opportunity you'll have to do this in any particular company. Being able to listen attentively is also of critical importance during the interview. If possible, try to find a course that videotapes you in an interview situation so that you can observe your unconscious mannerisms, body language, how well you maintain eye contact, and so forth.

Go for some informational interviews early on. Ideally, of course, you'd know what kind of job you're after and you'd choose those courses that would most boost your chances of getting it. This is really not such a difficult task, assuming that you're currently employed (or otherwise have no problem paying the rent) and are not under time pressure. Once you've had a few informational interviews with people in local companies, you'll have a better idea of what background you'll need. For example, many high-tech companies furnish each of their employees with a desktop computer, usually networked. And these are usually not PCs, but something more powerful, such as a workstation. It will be helpful if you can present yourself in job interviews as being familiar not only with PCs, but also with workstations, their user interfaces, and (say) their graphics capabilities. Of course, it's best if you can say that you've worked with the particular company's own machines, and sometimes this is a specific requirement. But if you're familiar with one type of workstation, it's not too hard to go to another, and what many people have done is to get familiar with Company A's machines in the few days between the time they find out about the job opportunity and the time they apply for the job. They sometimes do this through the contacts they have developed within Company A itself through networking, and sometimes through users' groups. Five hours with a particular machine can give you the confidence to look a hiring manager in the eye and say, "Yes, I've used your systems."

To summarize, if you're not at all familiar with computer technology, do the following:

1. Get a computer with documentation and learn how it works.
2. Consult a glossary and learn the terms relating to your computer.
3. Join a user's group.
4. Take a couple of courses.
5. Acquire interviewing skills.
6. Go for some early informational interviews.

Getting some high-tech background requires you to spend a few dollars and to invest some time. The payoff is that you'll have fun, you'll forget that you were ever afraid of technology, and you'll increase your chances of landing a great job.

Identification of Opportunities

There are four possible ways of getting into high-tech positions when you've been out working a few years. They are cold approaches, responding to advertisements, temping or contracting, and networking.

Cold Approaches

This is when you get a list of companies and broadcast your résumé as though you were an ancient Sumerian sowing grain. Of course, you don't just mindlessly mail your résumé. You get together a list of companies, get the names of the presidents, and send each one a letter with a résumé asking, in effect, for expressions of interest in hiring you. In the days when jobs were plentiful (back in the mid-1960s, for instance), the theory was that the president of the company, not being personally interested in your case, would pass your letter and résumé down to the HR department (in those days known as the personnel department). The personnel department would pay more attention to your résumé because it came from above, not through the U.S. Postal Service.

As you've gathered from reading the first part of this chapter, such an approach would seem to be extremely naive in today's job market.

Having said that, here's the experience of a woman who is an international marketing manager for a well-known software company. She is European, has an undergraduate degree from a European university, and started her job search in the second year of her MBA program at a large midwestern state university.

> I started with Standard and Poor's directory. There were a couple of drawbacks [to my job search]. One was that I was trying to get a job in California from the Midwest. The second was that as a foreigner I didn't have a work visa. So I decided I could only get results if I put a lot of work into it. I did about two to three months' research at the library on companies, and I gathered altogether maybe 500 names and addresses of these companies. Then I narrowed it down to about 270, using the product, the size of the company, their management. For example, did they have women in management. Also their location and whether they had international operations.

> I sent a mailing of a cover letter and a résumé to all these companies. I said that I would be in California on a certain week and that I'd be available for an interview. Then I did a telephone follow-up to approximately 150 of those. And I did get twenty interviews for the week.

> After these interviews, I followed up and got some second interviews. And by spring break I had another set of companies which was much more narrow, maybe around seventy, where I had followed up with letters or sometimes phone calls. I got around fifteen interviews at spring break.

> Out of these companies, two or three were interested. One of them flew me back. I did get two job offers. So by mid-April [of 1988] I did have a job. It was a small company, and I was the first marketing person on board.

Here is a case where the unexpected happened. If you have the time and are a methodical person, you can conduct such a campaign, and maybe you'll be successful. You be the judge. The chances are that this would not rule out your using other approaches to the same companies. The flood of applicants is great, and HR memories are short.

Responding to Advertisements

Strangely enough, it's often rather difficult to find out exactly what the requirements are for jobs in the high-tech industry. This is especially true if you found out about the job through a newspaper ad. Not only may the language used to describe the position be unfamiliar to you, but because these ads are expensive, not much detail is included about the work itself. Of course, if it's the sort of job you've already done, you'll recognize the word cues and feel comfortable about responding. On the other hand, there is liable to be too much detail of the kind that leads you to exclude yourself from consideration. That's why looking at the ads is usually a depressing experience—you think you've found some-thing that fits, and then bop! there's the kicker: "five years' experience" doing such and such, or "M.B.A. preferred."

One of the things to remember about hurdles of this sort is that the HR people have sometimes encouraged the hiring manager to insert them in an attempt to build in some sort of prescreening, not because they are really important for the job. Thus, if you can present yourself in a powerful and intriguing way, you can often circumvent these "re-quirements." This means being able to show the hiring manager that you appreciate the complexity and importance of the position, that you clearly bring to the table those fundamental skills that are required to do the job well, and that you are quietly confident of your ability to grow rapidly in the job to take care of any ancillary requirements. Gaining the trust of the hiring manager is worth virtually everything. If you meet the basic skill level of the position *and* the hiring manager thinks you can do the job and likes you, you have won.

On the following page is a real-world position description as it was published internally in a large software company. Note the require-ments set forth under "Competencies" and "Experience." This would appear to be a position for which a nontechnical person simply wouldn't qualify.

The position went unfilled for several months, until finally it was filled by a person with a nontechnical background, who did not speak Japanese, and whose knowledge of UNIX was picked up exclusively from work experience. This person's undergraduate major was govern-ment. The hiring manager stated during the interview process: "As usual, I was looking for a Superman or Superwoman. What I really want is someone who's smart, can learn, and is culturally sensitive."

But in many cases, especially for jobs advertised in the very expen-sive newspaper display ads that are used by the larger employers, the very technical people really are required; it's not a case of HR putting hurdles in your way. You'll recognize such cases because they will al-ways require a type of college or graduate degree you haven't got.

Now remember, there are many ways into the high-tech world. The largest high-tech companies, those that are constantly mentioned in ar-ticles in *The Wall Street Journal* and the business section of your local

POSITION PROFILE

Date: February 12, 1993

Position: Program Manager 3/4
Asian Locale Business Management
Software Localization

Purpose: Develop and manage business process for Asian and Japan localization centers.

Responsibilities: (location: USA with 25 percent travel)

- Develop and implement business plan for Asian locales.
- Develop and implement vendor management processes for Asian software and document translations.
- Develop vendor base for translations and delivery of localized software and documentation.
- Manage and secure technology acquisitions required to meet local market requirements.
- Develop and implement third-party programs and strategic partnerships required to support local market.
- Interface with marketing and sales to develop local market, customer, and product requirements.
- Support infrastructure for Japan and Asian localization centers.

Competencies:
- Must have strong leadership, communications, negotiation, and organizational skills.
- Must have proven record of accomplishments in intercompany business development, including technology acquisition.
- Must have proven record of accomplishments in managing vendor programs for software products and services.
- Must have thorough working knowledge of UNIX.
- Must have strong negotiation skills.
- Must be fluent in Japanese.

Experience:
- Minimum of five years' software industry experience.
- BS in computer science or equivalent; MBA preferred.
- Experience in software internationalization or localization preferred.

paper, are usually more difficult targets for the nontechnical person seeking his or her first job in the industry. Some of them grew too large and unwieldy in recent years, and missed market signals that they were in trouble; companies such as IBM, Digital Equipment, and Apple are actually reducing their workforces radically. They are hiring, if at all, for very specific technical functions; you'll rarely, if ever, see ads for non-technical positions. Former employees of such companies, as well as cur-rent employees who are fearful of losing their jobs, deluge the large firms that are in good health with résumés. So there is a lot of potential competition out there.

When you are looking for a high-tech job through classified ads, therefore, it can be much more rewarding to look for ads placed by com-panies that provide services to the larger, better known high-tech com-panies or that serve as sales channels for high-tech products. Don't ig-nore them just because their ads are small. These companies may be more impressed with your background than their larger, more blasé sib-lings in the high-tech world. And you will be accumulating valuable experience for your next move, be that within the same firm or to an-other company. A woman who is now in sales support in a large soft-ware company got her start in just this way:

> I saw a tiny ad in the paper for an electronic component sales company, and that's how I got my first sales job. It was also my first introduction to anything high tech. Why was I hired? I like to think of myself as being intelligent and articulate and very upbeat, and they must have recognized in me the capac-ity to learn.

And learn she did, thereby positioning herself for a move to her present job:

> The vendors would come in on a weekly basis and do train-ing, and I called vendors on a regular basis and asked ques-tions. I also took a course in basic electronics to become fluent in the terminology.

Between the very large companies, where it's hard (but not impos-sible) to get started, and the smaller sales and service firms, there are a very large number of midsize companies in the hardware, software, component, and networking businesses. Usually the strong growth is to be found in the healthy software and networking companies. Profit mar-gins on computers and their components are becoming slimmer every year, which is why these companies are seeking to reduce their costs, including payroll, any way they can. So check out the software industry.

You should always look at the ads to see which companies are hiring, and you should scour the smaller ads just as carefully as the larger ones. Sometimes you do find something interesting, and it looks as if there might be a fit. How do you verify this?

Well, you can't if it's a blind ad. And even when the company is identified, there's often a line in there that says, "No phone calls." Well, a few years ago, my family held a garage sale. We had an ad in the local paper that gave the hours of the sale. I think we planned to open up around eight in the morning. By seven-thirty most of the good stuff had gone; the antique dealers had come and picked up the old rattan furniture and discolored mirrors, and a few ordinary citizens, veterans of the garage sale routine, had taken the kids' old desks and dressers. They didn't obey the rules we had set, and so they beat out everybody else. Did we turn them away because it was being unfair to take their money at seven-thirty rather than eight o'clock? Will the Boston Red Sox ever win another World Series? So maybe a little aggressive marketing of yourself is in order.

If the company is in your vicinity, you can always drive over and try to charm the receptionist into giving you the name of someone working in the functional area where the job opportunity is located, to whom you can speak. That will sometimes work, especially in smaller companies, and especially if you can claim with a straight face that you've driven an hour and that you really feel you've got the right stuff for the job, but don't want to bother them with a résumé unless there really is a pretty good fit. This is a serious suggestion. Why not visit your prospective employer? At least you can learn the layout of the lobby. Maybe you can arrange to get there at lunch time and the receptionist can call someone over as the crowd leaves for the local deli. You might even get a free sandwich out of it. You can't tell what will happen, and occasionally what happens is nice. And since a little pushiness is valued, there is never a backlash to this kind of bold approach.

Or you can bend your energies to finding someone who works in the company, in *any* department, who might serve as an insider for you. This is sort of backwards networking—you've found the opportunity (you think), but you need to get more information, and you need to get known within the walls, even if you can't definitively breach them this early in the game. The problem is that you don't have a lot of time; the ad has been in the paper, and hundreds of letters and résumés are accumulating in a pile somewhere in the HR department. These days hundreds of résumés really do result from a single ad, particularly if the job is of a nontechnical nature. What you're really trying to do by hanging around the company that placed the ad is to make yourself stand out in any way short of setting fire to the place. If you can get inside, you might be able to accomplish this.

The Killer Letter

If you can't get inside, then the only way is to research the company as thoroughly as you can in a couple of days, then write a "killer letter" to go on top of your résumé. I don't think you should wait a few more days in the hope that your letter will stand a better chance of being read if it avoids the crush. By that time the folks that read applicants' letters may be in a glassy-eyed torpor, too dazed to operate a letter opener, much less accord the proper attention to your message. I think you should send it right off, but make sure that your cover letter will wake up the reader. To do this, cover letters should be short (not more than three short paragraphs), crisp, and have a grabber. A grabber is a line that will make the reader stop and take notice. A cover letter's sole purpose is to serve as a life jacket for your résumé, to keep it from being submerged in the tide of paper inundating the HR offices. *The substance doesn't matter so much as long as it gets you noticed favorably.* For substance you should limit yourself to one item from your résumé, the strongest and most relevant you have; you can allude to additional experience, but don't repeat your résumé and don't use tired phrases such as "my many years of experience in marketing." When it's at all possible, and above all with smaller companies, try to follow up by phone.

Here are three ways you can grab the attention of the HR person:

1. *Mention the name of someone in the company.* It might be someone you met, or it might be an officer who was mentioned in the press recently (you can get this information by checking resources at your local library). An example:

> I have been very interested in working for ABC Company since reading the speech given by John Markham [the president] at the Chamber of Commerce meeting last July. ABC Company seems to be at the leading edge of multimedia technology, and I would like to use my five years of PR experience in this exciting and dynamic environment.

2. *Ask for an interview to complete your research on the company.* Certainly, if you sit back and wait, you might get a call for an interview, but being a little aggressive can't hurt:

I've learned a great deal about ABC Company's general business through researching the business press, and I know your new line of disk drives is enjoying great acceptance in the market. I am convinced that my writing skills can help increase sales, and would appreciate it if I could have the chance to meet briefly with someone in your technical writing department so that I could present my experience, and see how it can fit in.

On letters like this, you should follow up with a phone call to HR, and ask to talk to the person handling responses to the ad. The operator will tell you that no phone inquiries are accepted. You should respond that you have already applied and that you are following up on your written request for an interview. Operators don't like to spend a lot of time handling inquiries like this, and you are likely to end up talking to someone from the HR department. This person, of course, will not be able to find your letter and résumé (unless it has been entered into a database); you should offer to send a copy of the original package. Since you now have the *name* of someone in HR, you should try to deliver the copy of the letter and résumé *personally*, and parlay this into the desired interview.

3. *Offer to work as an unpaid intern.* If you're currently unemployed, and after researching the company, you really feel there could be a good fit, this can sometimes be a winner. At the least your résumé ought to make the first cut. It can take a company weeks, or sometimes even months, to fill a position, yet the hiring manager has work that has to be done now. Why not have you do it?

I realize that you will probably have many replies to this ad and that it may take some time to review them all. The job appears so right for me that I am willing to work for ABC Company as an unpaid intern, with no strings attached, until you settle on the person you want to hire.

This approach can be more effective after you've had the first round of interviews, because your statement that this is the dream match is more credible after you've actually been in the firm and met some of your future colleagues.

There are books on the market that cover the "killer letter" idea quite thoroughly, and your local library or career guidance center undoubtedly also has one or two. And remember, when it comes to your cover letter:

1. Keep it brief.
2. Use a grabber.
3. Lead from strength.
4. Do phone followup.

Temping or Contracting

The Temp Agency

If you remember your medieval French history (and who doesn't), the supposedly impregnable fortress of Mont St. Michel on the Normandy coast was taken when a traitor let down a wicker basket from the ramparts one night and hauled up a bunch of English soldiers. These in turn opened the gates and let the army in. Well, the temp agency can accomplish, and rather easily, the task of getting you up the ramparts and inside the walls of high tech. These outfits have greatly expanded their high-tech operations in recent years in response to the downsizing of the large computer companies. They provide a way for experienced workers who have been laid off to get an income stream, but they are also an excellent channel for nontechnical people looking for their first job in the high tech industry.

Of course, these are often temporary jobs, and what you want is a permanent job. No, stop! What you want is a bunch of things, including income, some benefits, a good opportunity to learn, and (most important) *a chance to network within the high-tech walls.* And here are these outfits set up to do just that! It can be a nice arrangement. A manager of a growing software company in the Northeast told me

> We use a fair amount of contract and temp help because we
> can't hire fast enough.

Then why shouldn't you just apply for the full-time job, if they're hiring so fast? Sure, you can and should do that, but you should also go through the temp agency *because there is little or no competition.*

Temp agencies serving the high-tech industry often do so through two separate divisions, a technical division and an office services division (the names may vary). When you first approach a temp agency as a nontechnical person looking for a professional (nonclerical) position, you may find that the interviewer for the agency will be confused about which camp to put you in. He or she (usually she) won't want to put you in with the technical people, but may also feel that you don't belong with the office workers either. There are three ways of handling this situation.

1. *Go to more than one agency.* In fact, call all the agencies in your locality and register with all that claim to serve the high-tech industry. Temp agencies are like real estate offices—they are nationally advertised but locally controlled, and your reception and how you are treated will depend a lot on the individual with whom you deal and the particular relationship the office has with the high-tech companies.

2. *Be open to technical-sounding jobs the agency finds for you.* Often there will be entry-level jobs dealing with customers on the phone. If the company is sound and has a decent reputation (and you can discuss this frankly with the agency representative), don't hesitate to go after the job. Remember, what you need is high-tech credentials, and this is an excellent way of getting them.

3. *Be open to (some) office jobs.* Everything should depend on whether the company is expanding, standing still, or contracting. You only want to get involved with a company that has good prospects for survival and growth. If the temp agency can get you an interview as an admin in a software company that is growing like Topsy, and you like the people you'd be supporting, then it's well worth looking at. If the admin position is at DEC or IBM, forget it. If the position is doing filing, but it's for a startup company and you like the people, take it. If the startup is successful, you may be able to retire young. And even if the company grows only moderately, the chances are that you can expand into a better job within a relatively short period of time.

The temp agency rarely if ever really understands the full requirements for the job it has recruited you for. This can work to your advantage. When you show up on the doorstep of the hiring company at 9 A.M. Monday morning, the manager has no way of knowing anything about you until you start to perform. She or he will derive an initial impression of you based on your personality, how you're dressed, your energy, and other things you have direct control over. Even if you may not fully fit the company's requirements, by the time the manager finds that out, a week or more may have gone by, the manager's used to seeing you there, and you may even have volunteered to do extra work after hours because of your rapidly growing interest in the business. You can give the impression that you want to learn, to participate in the excitement, to grow as a (you hope) future member of the team. Having someone that motivated is almost irresistible to a hard-worked manager. And if it doesn't work the first time, it will the second.

The Contracting Agency

The essential difference between the temp agency and the contracting agency is that you become an employee of the temp agency and it usually gives you some benefits. When you are a contractor, the contracting agency usually just lines up the deal for a fee. Temping tends to place people at the lower end of the income scale, such as administrators and other office help and folks that work on the loading dock. Contractors tend to have some sort of specific skill that the company needs for the moment, say for the duration of a particular project.

A while back, high-tech companies thought that they could dump lots of individual contributors and then take them back as contractors, thereby saving the 25 percent or so of the total compensation package that goes for benefits. But substantial legal pitfalls lie in wait for such firms. If a contract employee is in all respects treated as if he or she were a full-time employee, except for being denied the company's normal benefits package, the company might be forced (through a lawsuit) to make the contractor a true employee. As a result, employers have to be very careful about how they hire contractors. It has to be a real arms-length deal, or it can end up costing the company a bundle.

This can make it more difficult for you to go from a contract position to being a full-time employee, but if you do get such a position, it may enhance your chances of getting taken on as a regular employee in another company because you will have gained the experience you need. And there is always the chance that you *may* be able to come on board with your contracting company. That, of course, involves getting on really good terms with your boss and coworkers, and ideally becoming Mr. or Ms. Indispensable. That's what happened to a woman who recently turned a contracting position in customer service into a full-time job. She said:

> Actually, the original position was a contractor. They brought me in to interview for the position, and it was telephone support. It wasn't exactly what I wanted to do, but I was willing to take it because I wanted to get into the company. In a couple of months they decided to make the job a real one.

Some of the professional nontechnical employees who were laid off by large companies in recent years began as individuals contracting their services, and now have started companies of their own and are marketing their services to the high-tech industry. While many of these companies are very small (one or two people), some, particularly in the training and management development fields, are larger and are growing. Such companies may be sources for employment in areas such as course development, training, communications skills, and sales. Other areas where new companies are being created to serve the high-tech industry include professional and technical employment recruiting. For some people, the way into high-tech starts by joining a temp or contracting agency as a recruiter, then acquiring additional credentials through a local college, and finally moving into a professional job such as HR specialist in a growing high-tech company.

Temping as an Admin

I know I've advised you not to be too picky about where you start out in high tech, because of the opportunities to move about once you're inside. But there's one possible exception to this, and that involves office workers. In the high-tech industry there are precious few of these, and normally the job is call administrator (admin) or some title other than secretary. No one in the high-tech industry seems to be a secretary, perhaps because very few letters are ever written—everything is done on the E-mail system or by phone. Still, once you are an admin, it can be very difficult to break out of that slot into an entry-level professional position. The reason is that *every* admin in the company is trying to do the same thing. So a lot will depend on the group you work for. Admin temps have ended up being marketing managers, they have ended up being technical writers, and they have ended up quitting in frustration. The best place to be a temp is in a startup or small but rapidly growing company, working for congenial and supportive people. These people will value you for who you are and the extra help you give them when the going gets tough. They will make a place for you in the permanent organization. The worst place to be a temp is in a department of a large company that is peopled with ex-military rednecks who pull rank at every opportunity, never invite you into meetings, and don't see any value in educating you in the business. A woman in her thirties told me:

> In [her former company], being a self-starter got you nowhere. It was a defense contractor. What was impressive there was how old you were, how much gray hair you had, how long you had been with the company. Those were the things that were more important—old line, the old boy network. Get up and go didn't help you a whole lot, and being a female didn't help you at all. When I came here, I felt I could make a contribution.

The nice thing about being a temp in a lousy situation is that it won't last too long—you'll move on to another assignment, and after the rednecks it's got to be a lot better.

Networking

Of all the techniques used to get a first job in the high-tech industry, networking is by far the most effective. It's effective for your second and third jobs as well; in fact, it's a technique that you should practice throughout your career in high tech.

A senior vice-president of a Fortune 200 high-tech company told me

> If I look at my own career, luck of course comes in from time to time, obviously, but apart from that my network has helped me the most, I would think—the relationships I built along the way. It's very true in our industry—there's an HP network, a Prime network, a DEC network, and I guess there's an IBM network. So very often when it comes down to filling jobs, people are asked, Do you know anybody who can do the job? Our president, that's the way he fills the positions, he goes to his board members and his staff and asks them if they know anyone they've worked with in the past who could do this job. More jobs come this way than from recruitment agencies. After all, these agencies rely themselves on the same networks.

> So it's all about who you know. And the network tends to be trusted because if you're referred, then you're a known quantity because the person who refers you knows that his reputation is on the line. My own key moves were influenced by the contacts I had. Positions were suggested to me that I might be interested in. You've got to build associations with your peers. The loners very often can go just so far, and they fizzle and fail. Because when the going gets tough, the network . . . it may not be right, it may not be fair in some cases, but it will keep an eye out for you. At this point networks are essential to a career.

As we've seen, going the classified ad route, while it must be pursued, is fraught with difficulties. You can control the process only to a limited degree. Also, it's here that you have the most competition. There has to be a better way, and there is. Networking is the way to go; in a minute you'll learn how to go about it. Networking properly executed is the Ponzi financial pyramid scheme redirected to the job market, with you as the exclusive beneficiary. It takes time, it takes organization, and it takes energy, but it really does pay off. And the delightful thing is that you are in control of the process every step of the way. The networking process opens doors that remain closed to others, and it can get you in front of a hiring manager *after* you have not only researched the job, but done so through conversations with your future colleagues. This gives them a chance to check you out, and vice versa. It gives you the chance to establish a connection with an insider, someone who will look out for your interests and coach you on what to do and say, and where the pitfalls are concealed.

A senior manager in the HR department of a very large company considered the question of how people could make contacts from the outside into the high-tech industry. She said:

> So how do people make contact with companies? There are the formal channels, but I also think there are the informal connections—friends, who you know. That's how people weave their way in. And I do think that [hiring managers] like to have a contact.

A woman who took a position in the training department of a company stated:

> From retail management to high tech, I knew somebody! That's how you find 85 percent of your jobs.

Having an insider contact makes you credible to the hiring manager, for the very simple reason that some of your contact's credibility rubs off on you. A woman who is now a vice-president of a software company spent some years working in state government as a human resources consultant.

> Then I decided I really wanted to get into the private sector, which is very difficult to do. But because I had been consulting, I had some clients in the private sector for whom there was some credibility. After a while one of them asked me to come in. I was lucky—it's awfully tough. The private sector is really skeptical of the public sector.

A friend of mine who had been working in the public sector for a few years decided to seek greener pastures. Here's how she started out:

> I went to the Career Resource Center in Palo Alto. Part of the membership is a three-hour appointment with a career counselor. So I made my appointment and I walked in and she had out her Magic Markers and pens to do tests, and I told

her to put it away, I had an agenda. So she said, 'OK, what is it.' I said, 'First of all, I want three names from whom I can get informational interviews so that I can get started. Second, I want to know what to wear for the interviews in Silicon Valley.' So we spent some time talking about that. I got my three names and she told me to dress like Barbara Walters.

I wanted some names. I didn't want to have to cold call. It scared me to death. So I had three names and I could start. I damn near got a job offer on the first one. And everywhere I went I got three more names. It's a pyramid. So you can continue meeting people. That was the only way I could think of to get a job.

I had a whole spiral notebook, and I kept the names and the notes on the interviews, directions on how to get there, and what happened, when I'd written the thank-you notes, all kinds of things.

I met a woman who was a recruiter for one of the chip companies. She and I talked for a little while. She ended up leaving her job at [Company A] and ended up at [Company B]. We became friends. She called me one day and said she had a job for me, to get my ass over there right away. So I did. This was about six months after I started.

You know, I hadn't been interviewing for jobs at all. They were all informational interviews. In some cases they resulted in leads for jobs.

How do you start your network? Starting with someone in the high-tech industry helps, but it isn't necessary, because everyone knows someone who knows someone who works in this industry. If you've just arrived in town and really don't know anyone, I suggest that you join a health club and get to know the members. You can be sure that some of them come from the high-tech industry or know someone who does. If you can't afford the fees, just ask them to let you put a notice up on the members' board with those little tear-off phone numbers on it. Explain in the notice that you need ten minutes of someone's time for an informational interview. All you need is one reply. (Your social life may pick up as well.)

Professional and alumni associations are also great places to start, as are outdoors organizations such as bicycling and hiking clubs. Professors who teach computer courses will be delighted to give you names, especially if you have been thoughful enough to enroll in their courses before asking. They are just as interested in networking as you are, since it is likely that much of their next European vacation will be funded through consulting to high-tech companies. And don't overlook the sorts of groups that read aloud from the Great Books. There's a Shakespeare group in Silicon Valley totally made up of high-tech worshipers of the Bard. Dentists don't have much to offer, although dental hygienists can be great sources of names. Chiropractors and orthopedic surgeons usually can produce a name or two, but often members of these professions have so little time for you, and so much of that is taken up with excoriating the others' profession, that you may be hard pressed to get the information you need. Also, you may run into issues of confidentiality here.

You get the picture—you can start a network anywhere. The keys to successful networking are to be organized and to *follow through.* If you get two names from one of your contacts (and don't leave the premises until you do), write them down in your job hunt records, and call those people as soon as you can. From each person you talk to, you should get two or three additional names of people in the high-tech industry or in professions that deal with high-tech companies. If you are disciplined and work at it, you'll acquire a list of contacts that will be extensive and unique.

The whole aim of networking is to start out by gleaning information, collecting names, and learning who's who, and either to end up with a job offer or, more likely, to find out from one of your contacts that someone in her division expects to have a job opening in the next few weeks, either because that function is expanding or because someone is leaving the company or otherwise moving on. This is precious information, because you are (you hope) the only person in the whole world outside the company who knows it. When that happy moment arrives, there's one thing you *must* keep in mind: Don't stop the networking process. Even if the position is so tailor-made for you that it fits like a glove, keep plugging along investigating all the other strands of your network, rigorously taking names and making notes. Because, as mentioned elsewhere in this chapter, the high-tech hiring process is often cloaked in chaotic mists, and strange things can happen. The hiring manager can get sick and die. He can also leave the company the day before he was to mail the offer to you (this is less forgivable than dying). Some Wall Street analyst can have a fight wth his wife, the next day he puts on a "hold" recommendation on the company's stock, it plummets, and a hiring freeze is announced. A rival manager gets his hands on the headcount. It goes on and on, and it has all happened before. So be optimistic, but keep your network alive and humming until the moment you get an offer letter.

When you get the offer letter, by the way, countersign it immediately, *make a copy*, take the original to the post office, and mail it return receipt requested. That way you've got a proven hiring date. High-tech jobs have been known to vanish after the offer letter went out, and managers have been known to deny receiving an applicant's acceptance letter. Not that this would ever be the case with *your* boss.

The Résumé

Here is a conversation with a man who has been in the computer industry for many years, and who has hired many people.

Q: How important is a résumé?

A: I don't consider it very important.

Q: Why not?

A: The information should be written there so that you're emphasizing your strengths, that's true. It is an information document. But in today's world the résumé is usually not read by anybody. It goes into the HR department and it gets scanned into a database, on which key word searches are done. It's a standard, canned program.

   And also this whole game of writing the résumé and putting it in the right way, with all the right words, is BS. Because most people don't want to tell somebody they don't have a skill . . . and it's usually [the lack of] all those social skills of communication that is why the person doesn't get the job. So people lean on their résumés, and then they don't get the job, and it's supposedly because of something that's not on their résumé. Hiring managers rarely tell them the truth: It's because you can't communicate very well. It's because I didn't like you when you came into the room. And you spilled coffee on my desk and you didn't apologize! It's that social, animalistic reaction that we have to another human being that decides whether we hire him or not. But the résumé will be used as an excuse.

Q: Does this system [HR scanning of résumés] work pretty well in your company?

A: No. [*laughs*] One of the reasons is that in this corporation, the reality is that each HR group doesn't communicate with the others very well. There's not the self-discipline to create a pool of information that can be shared across the company. The system ought to work well, but it doesn't. So it depends very much on whom you know, your references, being a good guy, all of that stuff. Word of mouth, friend of a friend, when people are looking for somebody. Somebody who can play with the team—that's the fundamental thing.

But not everyone thinks a résumé is unimportant. A young woman in a hardware company told me:

> By marketing yourself I mean taking time to do a résumé that looks good, to have a personal appearance and demeanor that makes sense in that environment, and then just showing some tact in how you communicate with the employer. Combining these things, you can sell yourself.

So what *is* the importance of the résumé? If you *must* go through the HR department to get to the hiring manager, it's critical. If the right buzzwords aren't on it, if your background doesn't seem to fit 100 percent, you're out before you get up to bat. A friend of mine who is a Hollywood actress told me once what it's like to go to an audition when there are a couple of hundred other hungry aspirants for the assignment. "The casting company has decided it wants a woman between thirty-five and thirty-seven years old," she said, "five feet seven tall, and with just such a shade of hair, cut in just such a way. If you're thirty-four or thirty-eight, or if you're five feet seven and a half, or if your hair is just a shade lighter or darker, they won't let you read. And this is for a spaghetti ad!"

That's what it's like sending a résumé through the HR folks when

Getting your résumés out.

you apply for a specific position. They've told you (though an advertisement) something about what they are looking for, but they haven't told you everything. Your résumé is your educated guess, and it's a long shot. If you have to go through HR, then you owe it to yourself to learn as much as possible about every requirement HR is looking for. This you can do only through talking to an insider, as outlined later in the chapter. Once you're armed with inside information, you can produce a résumé that has a much better chance of getting past the initial screening. A good rule of thumb is that for every advertised position not requiring a technical degree, there will be 200 external applicants, and HR will select five for passing through to the hiring manager. That's a 2½ percent likelihood of success. Inside information ought to improve the odds in your favor to 10 percent or better.

If you can bypass HR and can get directly to the hiring manager, the résumé is less important than the fact that you were recommended by someone the hiring manager knows and trusts. But it still has *some* importance. For one thing, if the hiring manager likes you, guess what? She's going to turn your résumé over to the HR people to include in their stack of likely candidates! HR people don't like to be bypassed, and are not above sniping at you through alleged gaps in your background or other "weaknesses." This isn't likely to be fatal, however. It's the hiring manager who's going to have to live with you, not the HR people. The worst they can do is to point out helpfully that Candidate Doe seems to be slightly better qualified for the job than you are. Fortunately, by the time they've done this, you've already made your second or third visit to the office to meet and be interviewed by others— your potential future colleagues.

Your résumé will be read by all of these people. In preparing it, you can consult many of the guides, but in any case you should adhere to these commandments:

1. Develop a separate résumé for *each* job opportunity. Keep track of which résumé you sent or delivered to which potential employer.
2. Put a job objective sentence at the top, right under your name and address. Put a single paragraph summarizing your skills and experience right under the job objective sentence.
3. Keep it to two pages maximum. One page is better unless you've got really stupendous qualifications for the job.
4. Make it easy to read—keep it clean, and use wide margins and good-quality white paper.
5. Make sure you highlight strengths, relevant to *this job*, rather than merely listing your previous work experience.

6. If you have had *any* high-tech exposure, put it in, using the proper buzzwords. That is, if you've used a PC, talk about being familiar with small systems. If you've taken a course, get it in, in five to ten words.

7. If you've been working for a few years, do a chronological résumé; use snappy, positive words that the hiring manager will be likely to understand. Never use jargon from your present line of work.

8. If you're relatively new to the workforce, use the functional type of résumé—what your skills are and what you've done with them, whether at work or in another setting.

9. Never use colored paper, perfumed paper, or a résumé cover, never include a photo of yourself, no matter how attractive you are. Never get fancy with italics or unusual fonts; it's *distracting*.

10. Don't mention high school, salary, family, divorces, references, or hobbies (unless you find out that you share one with the hiring manager).

The Video Résumé

An intriguing idea surfaced about two years ago: the video résumé. The candidate sends a videotape of himself to the prospective employer, along with the written résumé. In the videotape he talks for about ten minutes about himself, his skills and interests, and generally puts his best foot forward. If the position you are after involves customer contact, and you can get a tape made that will make you look professional, this approach would at least make your application stand out.

There are many pitfalls, however, and you should certainly have a disinterested party see the tape before you send it off. Many people look rather strange on videotape, and sound even stranger. That said, it's possible to get some assistance in the form of coaching from someone who's worked a lot with actors; such people are everywhere there's a community, university, or professional theatre company or drama school. The advantage of making a tape of yourself is that you can redo it as many times as necessary to get it right. If you can get a final product that you can show to your friends without having them burst out laughing, you've got something you can go with.

The Interviews

Before discussing the interview, I want to alert you to one thing you should keep in mind during every moment of contact you have with the people at the company you hope will soon be your company. This is the question of fit. You can have every attribute needed for the job, but if you don't have the fit, you won't get it. All that has to happen is for one member of the team you're seeking to join to say (in those very interesting meetings after you've gone home to sit by the phone, and your future is being discussed) that somehow, she's not sure, but she just doesn't see a good fit between you and the team. Then other people start to express doubts, and soon you're dead meat.

Fit is how people feel about you as a part of their system, to borrow the lingo of the psychologist, and that in turn depends on how you feel about them. So if you have some level of discomfort toward the end of the interview process, especially if things have otherwise gone well for you, bring it out and get it on the table for discussion in a diplomatic and nonconfrontational way. It could have been something you heard or saw; maybe some essential characteristic of the job seemed to be different from what you thought it would be. Or perhaps you thought you detected some hostility from one of the people who interviewed you. A good way to deal with this is to invite every person who interviews you to comment on the fit. They will appreciate it, and you will have the chance to clear up any misunderstandings and allay any doubts. This is a good way to solidify their commitment to you. Keep in mind that one or more of them may have had favorite candidates of their own for the position; but in virtually every instance they will at least admit that they could work well with you as a member of the team.

I suggest that you do a drive-by the day before you're scheduled to have your interviews. Check the place out. If you're fortunate, you've been able to get inside already, by charming the receptionist or some other stratagem. The easiest way, of course, is to use your insider.

But if you haven't been able to get inside, at least go to the place so that you know how to get there, and sit in the parking lot for a while. A friend of mine says she "just looked at the kinds of people leaving during lunch time" so that she would realize they were just plain folks, and she could easily work with them. It's just a means of relieving the tension a bit, like deep breathing.

Now to the hiring interviews themselves. These interviews tend to fall into three categories, so far as their structure is concerned, and which category yours will be in will depend very much on how qualified the hiring manager and others are as interviewers. Considering how many high-tech companies offer short courses for managers and individual contributors on how to conduct a hiring interview, it's surprising how many of them don't take advantage of them and still try to wing it.

The Chaotic Interview

I call the first kind of interview the chaotic interview, and it may start like this. You arrive at the hiring manager's office on time, hair combed and shoes shined, dressed like Barbara Walters or Bryant Gumbel (as appropriate; you should not under any circumstances engage in cross-dressing), and as prepped for the ordeal as you can be. And then the hiring manager doesn't show up for the interview—something important intervened and he didn't think to call you. Or he shows up half an hour late with one of his colleagues in tow, having a discussion complete with private jokes, while you hover in the background, smiling weakly and wondering whether this is all a ploy to take you off balance.

Never fear, it usually isn't. It's just the high-tech chaos well in evidence. In fact, it's usually a sign that you can control the interview, if it ever gets started. There are books that tell you in excruciating detail how to do this, so I'll just make a few observations. First, it's great (in fact, essential) to establish rapport. But in the chaotic interview, if you start out discussing your mutual interest in fishing, you are liable to lose control and end up spending the hour comparing the relative merits as bait of salmon eggs and nightcrawlers. The high-tech hiring manager who's not really certain of how to conduct the interview will usually take the easy way out, and whether it's Izaak Walton or Itzak Perlman who offers an escape (and it's rarely the latter), you may be sure he'll use precious time trying to take it. This is *your* interview, so keep the focus on the business at hand, even at the risk of appearing brusque. One more time: A degree of pushiness is respected in the high-tech industry.

You can ask lots of questions, but your choice of questions should leave no doubt in the interviewer's mind that you understand the job, where it is situated with respect to other activities in the department or the division, and how these fit into the big picture. Of course, if you are asked a question to which you don't know the answer, don't try to wing it. There are few dummies in the high-tech industry, and your interlocutor can spot a fake a mile off. In fact, your winning strategy for the interview has to combine enthusiasm for the job with what your unique contribution will be and what you hope to gain from the job in terms of self-development.

I suggest that you go into the hiring manager interview with a written list of questions and that you not leave without getting all the information you require. The questions should cover any lingering doubts on the part of your future coworkers that you sensed when they interviewed you. Usually these can best be raised in the final phase of the hiring interview, after you've made all the rounds. Of course, that means there has to be a roundup interview at the end of the day. Try like anything to make this happen. By then the hiring manager may well have talked to some of the others who've interviewed you. If any of them had doubts, you probably sensed them at the time, and if you couldn't resolve them then and there, you can address them with the hiring manager now. In the best of all worlds he'll say, "Oh, Tony's just jealous because he had a candidate for this job who's never gonna make it into *my* department!" And don't leave without asking that last, all-important question, one form of which is, "Do you feel that I have the qualifications to be successful in this position, or is there any additional information I can give you?"

The Scripted Interview

In this type of interview, the hiring manager is usually where she should be, behind her desk, and this time *she* is prepared with a list of questions. These are the questions that she remembers as being hard to answer when she was applying for a job, so why shouldn't she try them out on you? They're the kind that go, "What is your worst character trait?" or "Can you tell me a time when you really screwed up on the job?" These are, of course, very easy to answer once you anticipate them, but you should not make them appear easy to the hiring manager or you will disappoint her. The killer question used to be, "Why do you want this job?" Those of you who follow national politics closely may recall that the question was once asked of Senator Ted Kennedy on television, and at the time the job was president of the United States. Kennedy wasn't prepared with an answer. In the old days candidates usually had not thought very much about the answer, but realized that to blurt out "Because I need the money," or "I don't really want it that much, but I haven't yet heard from Company X on my dream job" would probably not be persuasive to the hiring manager. So there was a lot of stammering. Nowadays every candidate is prepped with replies that scatter buzzwords such as "challenge" and "development" (which I counsel you to avoid, as they make hiring managers feel ill). It's much better to say frankly that you know you can do the job well; you like dealing with customers, or engineers or whomever; you can hit the ground running; you see a terrific opportunity to learn; and you know you can relieve the hiring manager of some of the pressures on her. These are welcome sentiments.

The Job-Focused Interview

This type of interview is likely to be more demanding on you than either the chaotic or the scripted interview. Prior to starting the recruitment process, the hiring manager and the rest of the interviewing team have discussed job content exhaustively among themselves. The interview will be a team effort. They have decided what the particular skills are that are absolutely necessary for the work to be well done. Each of the prospective interviewers has a particular area to probe to see whether your background, temperament, and work history can really bring something to the job, and he or she is prepared with specific questions to which you must give specific answers.

A sure sign that you are engaged in such an interview is that the interviewer seems to be asking questions that do *not* naturally arise from what you've provided on your résumé.

How do you participate successfully in such an interview? First, be prepared. Review your work experience in the light of everything your research has turned up on the company and its style of work, as well as the job content. It's really important to arrange an informational interview or two for the days before the formal hiring interview. If you go into a job-focused interview without fully understanding what the requirements of the job are and what the work environment demands, you'll be at a serious disadvantage.

How many potential employers use this interviewing technique? Not many, even in companies where it is taught. The reason is that it takes time to execute a good job-focused interview. As important as the hiring process is, many managers simply do not take the time to set things up systematically on their end so as to be able to bring it off. It's just easier for the hiring manager to sit down with an HR representative for fifteen minutes and agree on a job description than it is to call together an unruly team and get them all to focus on job content and the skills and attitudes it demands. At one large company, 50 percent of all managers took a course that taught job-focused interviewing skills. Yet in that company the technique is actually applied only sporadically.

Coming to Closure

When you start closing in on a job opportunity, there are a few things you should be aware of if you are to keep from going mad. The first is that the process is likely to be long. Many high-tech companies are notoriously inefficient when it comes to adding a new person to their stock of their most valued asset. There seems to be an unwritten rule that to make this happen in less than three months would put a curse on the company. So be patient. Some people are lucky; they have a successful interview, and they're on board the next week. But much more typical is a series of delays that appear to the outsider to be absolutely inexplicable. These delays may come from the hiring manager's not being able to maintain the level of excitement about filling the position that he or she seemed to exhibit while you were being interviewed. Sometimes hiring managers get pulled toward other concerns and simply put filling the positions on the back burner. Of course, getting the job is what's uppermost in your mind, and you would like to think that this desirable outcome is uppermost in the hiring manager's mind as well. Usually it isn't, though, once you've left his office.

Since the process of getting applicants to fill a slot can be lengthy, it is also possible that while the hiring manager was busy making up his mind, others in the organization were reallocating headcount away from him. In other words, the job gets eliminated even as you are being considered for it. When the hiring manager finds out about this, he is naturally loathe to drop everything, pick up the phone, and inform you. For one thing, he still needs and wants the position to be filled; but now he has to do battle with HR, with competing departments, and with his manager. The process of rejustifying his need for the slot and denigrating everyone else's need, while not appearing to be greedy, demands both time and a high level of committment. One of these may be lacking. Also, the hiring manager, being only human, does not want to be the conveyor of sad tidings, and thus not only may not call you, but may never be there when you want to call him.

Another reason for delay in the hiring process is the HR function. Now the HR function exists in part to assist in getting good people into the organization, and for this purpose systems have been established to review résumés and screen applicants. As likely as not, however, the hiring manager ends up interviewing people who have circumvented these procedures. HR knows this very well. Because hiring managers themselves prefer to hire referrals, there may be just a soupçon of jealousy and resentment borne by HR people against the hiring manager, and they may well act this out using you as the punching bag. Here is the hiring manager who wants very much to get you on board. But the offer letter usually doesn't come from him; usually the process requires that it come from HR, which gives that department the chance to pass on your candidacy as well. Since HR is not independently qualified to judge your capabilities for actually doing the work, it tends to focus on process and on corporate concerns of which the hiring manager may be aware, but to the fulfillment of which he may not be totally dedicated. For example, has he leveled the job right? Are you perhaps a teeny bit overqualified? Underqualified? Has he considered all the corporate objectives with respect to the hiring of women, minorities, the physically challenged? Has the job been posted internally for the required period? And so on. Sometimes the hiring manager may find himself in a prolonged negotiation with an HR person on whether and how to bring you on board.

There may also—will also—be internal candidates for the job you're after. Some of these folks have had their eyes on it for a long time. They've been chatting up the hiring manager, working their way into his confidence, releasing those subtle pheromones to influence the course of events in their favor. And here you come at the last minute, threatening to destroy months of carefully constructed expectations and hopes! Better watch your back at the water fountain.

So how do hiring managers behave when push comes to shove? The fact is, they tend to go for the outsider, that is, for you. Something to do with the grass always being greener, if that's the metaphor. A veteran HR executive complained about this:

> There's no perfect person for a job. There's a sort of disease where you have a position and you interview a lot of internal people and most of them have made a mistake at some time or other in the past. Someone comes in from the outside in a brand new suit and they look perfect. And you tend to give them the benefit of the doubt.
>
> I personally would always go with the person whose defect you know. Because you *know* there are defects somewhere on the guy from the outside. You just don't know what they are. And in today's legal situation, doing reference checking in the U.S. is very difficult; unless you absolutely know and trust the person you get the reference from, you will always get a white bread reference. You will never really find out [what is wrong with the candidate].

Remember, the HR staff do not hire! They can try to derail an applicant, but the hiring manager controls the process and makes the decision.

All these currents and cross-currents are going on while you're sitting at home going over the interview process in your mind and wondering why the telephone doesn't ring. A propos of which, here's a tip: When things have gone very well during the final interview with the hiring manager, and all your future co-workers have assured you that they all think you're the greatest, it would be fun and rewarding to work with you, and they are looking forward to having you as a member of the team—when all this is in place, then you should not hesitate to bug the hell out of the hiring manager. This is no time to be coy. You want that job, and you deserve that job, dammit, and everyone agrees on that (except perhaps the aforesaid HR folks). You won't jeopardize your situation if you call the hiring manager two or three times a week to find out what the current status is. On one of those calls he's going to break down and level with you as to his internal problems in trying to get you on board, at which juncture you can sympathize with him and ask if there's anything else you can do to help things along. Usually there isn't.

Summarizing the Job Hunt

1. Remember the steps:
    - Do some self-appraisal and if necessary, make an attitude adjustment.
    - Acquire some background.
    - Identify the opportunities—network!
    - Target your résumés.
    - Get interviews with hiring managers.
2. Start anywhere; you'll move quickly.
3. The process may take three to six months; don't give up!
4. Have fun while looking, and keep your network alive!
5. Once you get on board, help other good nontechnical people by being part of a network.

4

Computers in
Ten Minutes

The purpose of this chapter is to get you feeling more comfortable about
working with people who have spent years in the computer industry.
I'm not referring to scientists and engineers who know all the bits and
bytes. Although you will have contact with such people, as a nontechnical employee you will not be required to understand the inner workings
of the microprocessor, the chip that really *is* the heart of the computer.
In fact, it's fair to say that many people in the industry, including some
in fairly technical positions, such as product managers, have no more
than a hazy conception of the chip's functions. Nor will you have to
know the deep technology of a network. Where you, as a new nontechnical employee, may run into problems will be in meetings or attending
presentations, where you'll hear terminology that you won't understand
or where allusions are made to trends in the industry of which you may
be ignorant. Not that anyone is going to poke fun at you for not knowing
these things; on the contrary, the people who work on the business side
of the high-tech industry are usually very understanding and willing to
help. When you first start working, though, it can be a bit overwhelming. Everyone except you seems to be so familiar with the industry; they
sling the jargon around with ease, and hold conversations with one another that are simply baffling to you. How can you ever break into this
charmed circle of insiders?

One thing you should keep in mind is that much of what you hear
and see is a display of surface knowledge, and that your colleagues, like
you, do not have to be intimately familiar with the technology. They
usually know what they need to know to do their jobs, and no more.
And the overwhelming majority of them picked up all their knowledge
on the job or through self-study or company-sponsored training, just as

you will. It doesn't take forever to get a handle on the technology, though it may seem an almost impossible task when you first start working. I hope that reading this chapter will give you a good start as well as encouragement to keep on learning every day. Everything you absorb from Day One will make you more and more comfortable with the technology and more and more of a valuable asset to the industry. I've highlighted the terms and concepts you're most likely to encounter during your first weeks on the job, and I've tried to get the meaning across by the context; where this wasn't possible, I've given the meaning in a footnote.

Some General Advice

Here is some general advice about acquiring knowledge about computers. First, get started now. Even if you're only contemplating a possible career shift, make learning a part of your career plan and start implementing it. If you have never worked with a computer, buy one. It doesn't have to be new, although if you buy a used one, you'll need to exercise some caution. John Bear's *Computer Wimp No More** is an amusing guide to buying and working with a personal computer, and contains a lot of useful information.

Once you get your PC, you should also buy one of the fat books that deals with your computer's operating system. Two recent good examples are *DOS for Non-Nerds*, by Michael Groh[†] and *The Apple Macintosh Book,*[‡] 4th ed., by Cary Lu. Books such as these really help demystify computers. Another step you ought to take is to join a user's group for your particular make of computer. These groups are everywhere—ask your local computer or software dealer. Members of user's groups are wonderfully patient when it comes to answering questions.

Next, when you are actually working in the high-tech industry, keep a notebook and write down questions as they come to you, at least to the extent possible. Otherwise you'll forget them until they return in some other context. When I first started in the industry, I'd attend presentations and feel pretty lost. I started scribbling down some of the more puzzling terms or issues and asking about them later. Which brings me to the next point: Please remember that *there is no such thing as a stupid question*. Or as the old saw has it, the only stupid question is the one you don't ask. When everyone around you is merrily discussing

---

*Ten Speed Press, 1992.
[†]New Riders Publishing, 1993.
[‡]Microsoft Press, 1992.

EISA buses, for example, and you don't know whether it's about computers or public transportation, *ask!*

Set aside some time each day, even if it's only half an hour, to read an industry publication or a technical specification sheet or some other document dealing with your company's business. Again, jot down concepts or terms that are giving you trouble. Then discuss them at lunch the next day; see what people have to say about them. If a topic really interests you, or if your company is heading in a particular technological direction, you can seek out your company's resident expert on the topic and have him or her at least point you in the right direction to dig more deeply into it. You will have to be sensitive to the time demands on these people, but if you succeed in lining up a coffee break or lunch with them, you can receive in a few minutes a real and real-time education that you cannot get in any course. "Real-time" in this context means that it's the state of affairs right *now*. One friend of mine who is a technical writer takes a tape recorder to these sessions; later she transcribes the tapes. She said:

> What I learned was that there were people disposed to help me because they liked me or because they knew that they needed to deliver some important piece of information for their own particular set of needs. So a lot of the time there was the belief that if they helped me, then they would be successful and I would make them successful, and that worked out really well.

And a young man who mans a hotline for a software company observed:

> One thing, I've been really fortunate to have good people to go to answer questions. Of course, when you ask the same question two or three times, eventually you do learn it. And so you ask bigger questions [*laughs*]. Of course, if you ask the technical people questions you could research yourself, you start taking advantage of that relationship, and then it's not so easy to get answers. Building relationships and really listening and learning and trying make a big difference. Because they respect you and take more time to really teach you.

Five Important Areas

There are five areas in the high tech industry with which it will be helpful for you to be conversant:

1. Computer families
2. Networks
3. Operating systems
4. Microprocessors
5. Industry jargon

When I say conversant, I mean that these are topics you should have some familiarity with as you start off. You'll feel more at home in the industry and more comfortable in your first days on the job if you do. But you'll feel very uncomfortable if you set yourself the goal of attaining in-depth knowledge right off. It just won't happen, and you'll start to feel discouraged. I guarantee you that within a year of your starting off in your high-tech career, you'll be surprised (and your friends outside the industry will be amazed) at how much new knowledge you'll have absorbed.

Computer Families

A few years ago it was fairly easy to identify a few discrete categories that included most types of computers. These were **mainframes, minicomputers, workstations, PCs,** and **laptop** and **notebook** computers. Now these didn't all come into existence at the same time. First came the mainframes, the great product of IBM in its glory days. Mainframes were huge machines that had to be kept in very large, specially air-conditioned, dust-free rooms and were tended like demanding gods by dust-free acolytes. These machines were surrounded by all sorts of whirring and clicking **peripherals,** such as tape and disk drives (and in the really early days, paper punch-card feeders) that fed data into the mainframe and printers that received the end product of the computer, printing it out onto **hardcopy.** Whole specialized data processing departments, with specialists who knew how to use the mainframes, grew up in large corporations. These departments developed specialized **applications software** to solve the particular problems of the business, be it scientific research, processing of loan applications, developing actuarial tables, handling personnel records and payrolls, determining the optimal time for planting bananas, or whatever. Data processing department employees would receive requests for assistance in solving problems from the company's other divisions. They would work with employees of these other divisions to scope out the problem and reduce it to terms the computer could understand. Back in the data processing department, they would place the problem in a queue to be worked on by the computer when its scheduled time came up; this was known as *batch mode processing.* (Getting time on the mainframe was often quite an issue in those days.) The data processing people would then feed the problem to the computer, get the answer, and report it to the "customer" within the company.

So computing, in the early days, was defined as a centralized function known as **MIS,** for management information system, within a company that was rich enough to afford the machine, the peripherals, the **programmers** to develop the specialized software, the contracts for maintenance to keep the machine going, and the managers to keep the whole department going. All this was roughly what computing was like in the 1960s. It placed tremendous power in the hands of the managers of the data processing centers because they could determine priorities and actually shape the information that the rest of the company would have to rely on for its operations. No one could gainsay them because no mere mortal could understand what was going on behind those dust-free doors.

Decentralization of Computing

In the early 1970s there was heresy about. A few bold engineers in a new company, Digital Equipment Corporation (DEC), developed a new kind of computer, which they called the **minicomputer.** Despite its name, today we would consider those early minis to be very large indeed—perhaps the size of a side-by-side refrigerator/freezer combination. But compared to the mainframe, the mini was very small. Minis were very powerful, were nimbler than the mainframes, and, most revolutionary of all, *decentralized* computing. Instead of work having to be brought to the data processing specialists, the power of the minicomputer was now brought to the people who really needed the answers, by means of **terminals** that actually stood on or next to their desks. The terminals were simply computer monitors, or screens, with a keyboard, so that data and instructions could be typed directly by the end user. The people using the terminals became part of a **distributed computing** network. They could use the computer without having to kowtow to the data processing manager. You could have several people each of whom would be using a terminal hooked up to the mini, and to each of these users it would seem as if he or she were the *only* user of the mini. That's how powerful these new machines were. Occasionally there might be a slight wait if some other user were doing a **compute-intensive** application. If you got too many users and the blips got to be too long, you could add a second minicomputer to the first—just hook 'em together and presto! you doubled your capacity and the blips went away.

There were lots of nice things about the minis. First, they were cheap compared to the mainframes, not only in initial purchase price but, even more important, in a concept called **total cost of ownership.** That's how much it would cost a company to keep one of the things going over its lifetime. Second, and contributing to the lower lifetime cost, minis had a smaller **footprint**; they still needed a cool, dust-free room, but it could be a small room. Space costs money. Next, it cost a lot less to maintain a mini; maintenance cost for mainframes were horrendously high. Many minicomputer sales were made by demonstrating to the customer that in as little as two years the cost of a brand new minicomputer system with terminals and cabling would be recouped by not having to pay maintenance costs on the old mainframe. And with a minicomputer installation you could add computing power as you needed it, instead of having to invest in a monster machine at the beginning. Having computing power at the desktop made teamwork possible between users on the system, whether in the same building, in different towns, or even in different countries. Finally, since computing was now decentralized, you didn't really need a whole specialized staff to control and manage it.

Minis got to be very popular, as you might imagine, except with managers of those central data processing departments, who began to have visions of ending up on bread lines. But for huge data crunching jobs, there continued to be a place for the mainframes. Some customers had a mainframe for some applications and minis for other applications. Of course, since both the **operating systems,** the basic software that wakes the computer up and tells it how to run through its paces, and the basic designs and standards of the hardware, or **architectures,** were quite different for the mainframes and the minis, it was not possible to hook these disparate systems together, at least not at first. The mini manufacturers spent a lot of time and research money trying to do this, because being able to tell a customer that the systems would all work together made a nice sales pitch. Finally this goal was achieved, at the expense of considerable complexity in systems configuration. In other words, you had to add more specialized equipment to bridge between computers from different manufacturers, and because of differences in the operating systems used by these manufacturers, it was just plain not possible to bridge between all types of computers.

The Personal Computing Paradigm

In the 1980s came the phenomenon of the personal computer, or PC. These robust little items didn't need a dust-free, air-conditioned environment; they were cooled by internal fans and could be used in an office or at home. And they were cheap! They initially stored data on removable **floppy disks,** so called because the disk itself (but not the envelope) is made of a flexible film. Floppies hold from 400 kilobytes to 1.4 megabytes. A 1.4-MB (megabyte) disk can easily hold a book the length of this one. Later the floppies got smaller and could hold much more data, and PCs began to be made with **hard disks** built right into them. The hard disks are really hard, as opposed to the floppies, and may be stacked on top of one another like tiny pancakes, with little spaces between them. They are mounted in sealed containers to keep out dust and other potential contaminants, and can hold millions of bytes of data—from 40 to 360 megabytes. The PCs displayed input and output on monitors, just as the terminals did for the minis (in fact, you could use some PCs as terminals for minis), and were hooked up to printers. The PC was responsible for the explosion of applications software, and the reason for this is the fantastic number of these machines that are out in the market and the fact that the vast majority of them all run the same operating system and are based on the same family of microprocessor chips made by Intel Corporation. In 1993 about 45 million PCs were sold that used the Intel chip and the MS-DOS operating system. From the start of the PC explosion to the middle of 1993, about $150 billion worth of software was sold to run on Intel-based PCs.

Today there are perhaps 15,000 applications, or **apps,** that run on top of the MS-DOS operating system. Computing has moved into small businesses, schools, and the home. The 1980s were really the decade of the PC. Sales of PCs remain strong, but the rate of sales growth has flattened out as the market has become saturated.

The Cooperative Processing Paradigm

In the middle of the 1980s the paradigm began to shift once more. A new type of computer, the **workstation,** emerged on the scene. In some respects the workstation looked like a PC. It was relatively small and relatively cheap (compared to a mini), and it stood on a desktop. But that was where the resemblance ended. This new type of computer was fantastically powerful and could therefore run applications on the desktop that were only dreams a few years previously—applications such as oil field reservoir simulations, medical imaging, telephone network management, three-dimensional design, currency trading, and software development. Its monitors had superb resolution in both black and white and color. Workstations were also capable of **multitasking,** which meant that you could pull up two or more **windows,** or displays on the screen at once and run one application on one or more screens while doing something else on another. And workstations were made to be **networked,** a feature that had a powerful effect on the way people worked within an enterprise. Networks linked users together; users could now share and exchange files directly, and two or more people could work on the same problem at once, sharing results. Also, audio, still photo, and video **multimedia** capabilities were built into the computer, thereby introducing new ways of transmitting information.

One of the main features of a computer system is its ability to hold data in storage by means of its internal **memory.** This kind of memory is different from the permanent memory provided by storage devices such as floppies. Workstations had plenty of **random access memory,** or **RAM,*** which meant that they could hold the ever-larger applications programs that were growing up like mushrooms after the rain, and huge amounts of storage capacity on their internal hard disks. But they could also work in cooperation with other, even more powerful computers called **servers.** Servers are computers whose purpose is not necessarily to do the computation (though some may be used for this), but to hold files and applications programs in storage until the workstation calls for them to be **downloaded** so that a user can work with them. Downloading the program doesn't take much time at all, since the servers are powerful and the workstations have plenty of capacity. This kind of relationship became known as **client-server computing.** Servers also offer special services to their clients, such as printing, file sharing, and database access.

This kind of computing got started in the technical and scientific communities in the 1980s, simply because scientists and technical users were naturally involved with extremely complex problems that demanded a lot of computing power, and it was ideal to have this power available on the desktop. Workstations stayed in the labs for quite a while, but then began to move into other professions where the problems demanded vast amounts of power. A stunning example is in the medical profession, where it is now possible for a surgeon to plan an operation such as reconstructive facial surgery, simulate it on a workstation, and observe the results before it is actually performed on the patient.

Now after all these players—mainframes, minis, PCs, and workstations—were on the computing stage, interesting things began to happen. For one thing, the lines between them began to blur. Minis had already started encroaching on the mainframes' turf in the 1970s; in the 1990s workstations and servers began to move into the minis' space, and

---

*Random access memory is the semiconductor memory in your computer that provides temporary storage for applications programs and output from your work. When you turn your computer off, the content of the RAM vanishes, which is why you must save your work into a permanent memory device, usually a floppy or hard disk.

down to the high-end PC. And high-end PCs began to look remarkably like low-end workstations. In an interview in April 1993, Scott McNealy, the chairman, president, and CEO of Sun Microsystems, said:

> Unfortunately, 'PC' is a conventional terminology. But I have no idea what a PC is. . . . There's several ways I segment the industry. . . . [One is] by where the product goes. Some product goes to the home, some product goes to the briefcase—the nomadic devices, if you will—and some product goes into the office. Then down the hall you have . . . servers.

Price wars break out from time to time in the PC world, and 1993 was no exception. Profit margins became so low that innovation started to become too costly. Similarly, the prices of workstations began to drop as more and more manufacturers began to get into the power desktop market. The emphasis was on saving costs, and hence on farming out manufacturing of components to the lowest outside bidder. **Product life cycles** became shorter and shorter—in workstations, new products that were twice as powerful for the same price, or that had the same power at half the price, emerged from the labs first every three years, then every eighteen months, and now every eight to twelve months. And there was a powerful impetus away from proprietary products and toward **open systems,** as already noted in Chapter 2.

Almost everyone is aware of the growth in popularity of laptop and notebook computers in the last two or three years. Such machines are the latest in the evolution of the computer that started with the "portable" PCs weighing twenty pounds or so that appeared in the early 1980s. It appears that the next genus of computer will be the **personal digital assistant,** or PDA. No one is entirely sure what these machines will be, but ultimately they will provide the user with wireless access to networks, voice and video capability, large memory storage, and cellular telephones, all in a lightweight machine that will perhaps be as large as a softcover mystery. Apple was the first company to put a PDA on the market, in August 1993. The machine is known as the Newton, and though its reception initially was mixed (critics claimed its price was too high and its usefulness too limited), Apple and other companies, including a host of startups, will surely be offering other products to fit this market space.

Networks

A network is simply the hooking together of **nodes,** each node being a computer or terminal, so that they can all communicate with one an-

other. There are various network **topologies,** or patterns, but these need
not concern us here. The important thing is that a person or group of
people can communicate easily with others, who may be ten thousand
miles away or in the next room or next building, even working simulta-
neously on the same problem, sharing information, exchanging ideas,
and, in short, working together. I asked a business manager to comment
on the importance of the network. He said:

> It's important to tie people together because people naturally
> work in groups—workgroups. People tend not to be islands,
> as John Donne said. The PC brought computing to individ-
> uals on a mass scale. It kind of forced people to change their
> working paradigms, to fit into one person, one computer. But
> now, for example, if I'm working with a purchase order, it's
> not really just me who's involved. There are maybe fifteen
> people who have to be involved—the workgroup. With client-
> server and networking that's become possible—to simulate
> the complete work flow. Purchasing is a good example. It af-
> fects accounting, invoicing, the movement of goods out of the
> factory, inventory, shipping—all that. There's a new kind of
> software that permits this. It's called groupware. It's software
> that enables a group of people to perform their normal inter-
> active functions in a collaborative manner.

There are various ways in which computers are hooked together
into networks. In a **local area network,** or LAN, the network is likely to
be an **Ethernet** connection. Ethernet is a standard adopted by the Insti-
tute of Electrical and Electronics Engineers, or IEEE. It's the oldest and
most widely used type of LAN, having been developed back in 1973.
You can see that it's necessary to have standards; without them, the
transmission of information might face the same kind of problem a train
does when it tries to go from Poland into Russia. Russian railroad track
has a wider gauge than that in the rest of Europe; therefore every car of
the train has to be jacked up and fitted with trucks that fit the wider
gauge. A Russian engine is hooked to the train, and off it eventually
goes. That might be all right for rail traffic, but it's not acceptable for
electronic communications.

But having said that, it should be observed that there is more than
one standard for LANs. In addition to Ethernet, for example, there's the
token ring network. It also conforms to an IEEE standard—a different
one. Token ring was introduced by IBM in the mid-1980s. The battle over
standards is a fascinating aspect of the computer industry, and it pervades not only hardware and networks but software as well. The expla-

nation for this is simple: Those who develop products that become industry standards have achieved a competitive advantage. The others have to give up what they've been working on and sign up for the standard. You'll have plenty of exposure to the standards wars as you pursue your career in the high-tech industry.

There are various kinds of cabling that Ethernet networks can use, from specially manufactured cable to already installed telephone lines. And the newest cabling doesn't transmit electricity; **fiber optic cable,** relying on another standard known as Fiber Distributed Data Interface, or **FDDI** (by which acronym it is exclusively known in the industry), uses pulses of light to achieve much higher transmission speeds without the problem of external electrical interference. FDDI allows high-resolution graphics and digital video to be quickly transmitted. But it's much more expensive than transmitting "over copper," that is, by wire.

So far we've been talking about local area networks. There's another type of network, called a **wide area network,** or **WAN,** that is used to span the entire globe. In a WAN the information may be transmitted in different ways. These include telephone cables and dedicated telephone lines, but by far the fastest-growing method is microwave transmissions relayed by satellites that can handle voice, data, and video. It's not at all necessary that you understand this technology; but it's something to wonder at. You can sit at your desk in Boston and send a three-dimensional technical design, complete with voice commentary and written notes, to a colleague in Singapore. When you come in to work the next morning, he's done his work and sent the project back to you. If one of you is a night owl, you can work together, exchanging ideas and testing each other's work as you go. Of course, you can include your friends in Germany or France as well.

There are many absorbing technical areas in networking that are really not difficult for a nontechnical person to understand; for example, in a LAN, why don't little bits of data keep bumping into each other? And there is a lot of opportunity to learn about these matters, by taking short courses in the company or attending seminars or just asking someone who knows to give you a short "chalk talk" in her office. Networks are without doubt one of the most important areas of the industry and will be for years to come. They offer a tremendous area for growth as all the islands of PCs in all the organizations around the world start to get hooked together. It's a great word to have on your resumé, and I suggest you look into it.

Operating Systems

As mentioned earlier in this chapter, an operating system is a piece of software that gets the computer to perform its basic functions. For example, it tells the computer to load application programs when you instruct it to do so. It manages the peripheral devices attached to the computer (tape and disk drives, the monitor, printers, the keyboard and mouse) through **device drivers,** which are parts of the operating system dedicated to such management. The operating system also acts as the intermediary between the applications program and all the data that program might require, which is stored either in internal memory or in an external storage device. When the applications program calls for a bit of data, the operating system scurries off to find it and delivers it to the program. And when the applications program comes up with a solution to whatever problem it's been working on, it hands this solution over to the operating system, which dutifully finds a safe place to store it—for example, on a hard disk.

Another very important function of some operating systems is that they permit the multitasking mentioned earlier; you can perform operations while the computer is working on another task you've set it to solve. The operating system also manages your system's security, limiting access to your files to those who know the correct password, and perhaps shutting down entirely if someone tries repeatedly to enter your files using wrong passwords.

The operating system is like the stage manager of a big Broadway musical: She's always there behind the scenes and things would grind to a halt without her, yet the audience (the users of computer systems) never thinks about her. The stars of the show (the applications programs) get all the applause.

Operating systems were developed by computer manufacturers as well as third-party developers, and there are many different ones in operation today. If you have worked with a personal computer, the chances are that it uses either MS-DOS (standing for Microsoft Disk Operating System); OS/2, developed by IBM; or the System used by the Macintosh (the current version is System 7). But there are several others, some of which are no longer manufactured (for example, CP/M). Larger computers likewise have their own operating systems, some of which are designated by groups of letters (for example, AIX, HP-UX, VM, VMS, and ULTRIX). It's not necessary for you to know what these initials stand for. What *is* important to know is that (1) applications programs are initially developed to run on a particular operating system, and (2) traditionally most operating systems have been **proprietary;** that is, they were developed to run on one manufacturer's computers, and those computers only. For example, assume that a software developer has come up with a terrific applications program for managing hospitals—everything from the scheduling of operations to the ordering of supplies, to the tracking of payroll, to monitoring the stocks of drugs. This program could, conceivably, reduce the costs of running a hospital by some 5 percent without affecting the quality of care. The developer has used a system running VMS to develop the hospital software, so ipso facto this application will run on VMS machines. But all the VMS machines in the world are made by one company, Digital Equipment Corporation. If a hospital happens to use a different brand of computer (say a large Data General machine), it cannot use the software developed on VMS.

Similarly, if I own software that will help me do my taxes, and it was developed for MS-DOS, it will not run on my neighbor's Macintosh. The applications software is not **compatible** with the operating system.

It's hard to fix responsibility for this situation, and ultimately fruitless. Manufacturers who created operating systems in the 1970s and 1980s obviously tried to develop systems that had unique attributes that would help them sell computers. And this incompatibility of operating systems certainly helped the profitability of these companies, in that once an enterprise purchased a particular brand of computer with its operating system, and then developed or bought software to run on it, it had to keep buying the same brand of computer so that the software would continue to be compatible on all of them. The enterprise was "locked in" by the operating system. If another computer company were to offer the enterprise a faster, more powerful, and cheaper machine, it couldn't buy it because its software wouldn't run. The people who developed software also faced problems. Software development is a very complex, tedious, and painstaking process, full of opportunities for errors, or **bugs.** Bugs ultimately have to be fixed, which may require a temporary **bug patch** or a new, improved version, a software **upgrade.** Developers want to be rewarded for their labors by selling lots of **software licenses** (permission to use the software under certain terms and conditions), but they're faced with the question of *what operating system to write the software to.* They have to decide whether to favor VMS (which benefits Digital Equipment Corporation), or VM (which benefits IBM), or HP-UX (Hewlett-Packard), or System 7 (Apple)—the list goes on.

The computer manufacturers all have programs to try to lure developers to write to their own particular operating system(s), because it is the applications programs that sell the computers, not the other way around. You might say that all the developer has to do is to count the machines out there and then choose the dominant operating system; that's how he can sell the most licenses and make the most money. True, and this is easy to do in the personal computer world, which is why any developer in his right mind writes programs that can be executed easily on a personal computer to (at least) MS-DOS and the Macintosh System. But the situation is not so clear in the case of the hospital management software. Which manufacturer's computers dominate the hospital management market? Or the oil exploration market? Or the retail chain dry goods market?

Applications software developed for one operating system can sometimes be **ported** to another operating system with relatively little fuss, requiring only a simple **recompiling** (i.e., using a piece of software, the **compiler,** to translate from one operating system to another). Sometimes this can be done in a single day. But sometimes weeks or months of work by a whole team would be required, and the developer may decide that the incremental sales opportunity just isn't worth the effort and expense (there are heavy costs associated with issuing a new **release** of the software for the new **environment**). In such a case, the manufacturer sometimes steps in with an offer to fund, in total or in part, the porting of the software to its systems, including offering engineers to help with the port.

It's obvious from all of the above that life would be simplified for the developer as well as for the consumer if there were only one operating system, or at least if there were some way to make applications run easily on more than one operating system. In fact, an operating system called UNIX that is able to run on a wide variety of systems was developed in 1969. But UNIX wasn't very **user-friendly;** using it required mastering complicated commands. Initially it had no **graphical user interface,** or GUI. That is the system of pop-up menus and icons on the computer screen that makes any software easier to use. UNIX found a home mostly in scientific laboratories and computer science faculties, where the technical staffs didn't mind its complexity. Some companies developed commercial versions of UNIX, but since its widespread use would have eliminated the advantage manufacturers got from locking customers into their own operating systems, and hence their own machines, they had little incentive to promote it.

Nevertheless, the pressure from end users, and notably from the federal government, to eliminate the problem of incompatibility grew, and when UNIX began to feature GUIs, and hence became much simpler to use, the fact that it was an **open operating system**—one that could support multiple manufacturers' computers in local and wide area networks (as opposed to the closed proprietary operating systems)—gave it an advantage, and it started to catch on in the commercial market. Certain large commercial users and some government departments may have many hundreds or even thousands of PCs on the desks of their employees. The majority of these run some version of the MS-DOS operating system and use a microprocessor chip from Intel Corporation. A current battle that is shaping up in the industry is to see which operating system will be successful in tying all a large corporate user's PCs together into an efficient network. MS-DOS lacks many features that would be required in such a network, especially multitasking (being able to run two or more programs at the same time) and being multiuser (the computer is able to be used by two or more people at the same time). UNIX supplies all these features, but used not to run on the normal PC*. Two major companies in the industry, Microsoft and Sun Microsystems, have developed competing operating systems to attempt to win this market. The new Microsoft OS is called Windows NT, for New Technology. Sun's new OS is called Solaris. And IBM and Apple have joined in an effort to create a third new OS called Taligent. It takes an immense investment to create a new operating system; Sun had over 1,000 engineers working for a year to create the version of Solaris that runs on both UNIX and Intel machines. The aim of this investment is not to get your home computer to run differently. The aim is to win the huge market represented by the world's largest enterprises, including government departments and universities.

The ultimate goal is compatibility and seamless **heterogeneous networking**—the tying together of all makes of computers, no matter whose microprocessor is inside. Ultimately this will happen, but not before there have been a few years of intense battles between the giants of the OS side of the industry.

The Microprocessor, or Bits and Bytes

Computers run on tiny amounts of electricity, which gets routed through the heart of the computer, called the **microprocessor.** If you can imagine a microprocessor blown up a zillion times (its actual size might be about that of your thumbnail), it'd look like a very complicated model railroad, with tracks running every which way, switches, turntables that could reroute locomotives onto different lines, signals to hold traffic, tunnels, drawbridges, and so forth. Instead of trains running along the tracks, though, what the microprocessor has is little bursts of electricity. The computer recognizes only two states of being, off and on. Or, if you like, a burst of electricity or no burst of electricity. We can represent this on paper by using a zero to show when there is no burst of electricity and a one to show when there is a burst. For example, 01 means that first there's nothing and then there's a little locomotive . . . er, burst of electricity roaring down the track. Each one of these states of being, or numbers, is a **bit.** That is, the zero is a bit, and the one is a bit.

How do we get from this simple stuff to having a computer be able

---

*Xenix™, a UNIX operating system from The Santa Cruz Operation, Inc., does run on "heavy-duty" PCs.

to, say, print the letter *a*? Leaving out a lot of useful stuff like the operating system and word processing software, and just getting to the heart
of things, we could arbitrarily string together a whole bunch of bits and
have them represent the letter *a*. For example: 00000001 might represent
an *a*. Or, for that matter, 00100101 could represent an *a*. For our purposes it doesn't matter, as long as we're consistent. So when we press
the *a* on the keyboard, that pushes a little train of electric bits down on
its journey through the microprocessor: off, off, on, off, off, on, off, on.
What we've done is send an eight-bit **word** on its merry journey. This
"word" is obviously not a word in the ordinary sense, but only in the
computer sense. Another name for this is a **byte,** which is a made-up
term for a bunch of bits, eight to be precise.

A bit is the smallest amount of information a computer can handle,
but it can handle all sorts of combinations of bits, and when computers
started out, they handled eight bits, or one byte, at a clip. This is why
you'll hear people refer to old PCs as eight-bit machines. Later, as computers got more powerful, they became sixteen-bit machines, and there
are many of these being sold today. These machines are much faster
than the old ones because the locomotives carry two bytes of eight bits
each.

Modern workstations are thirty-two-bit machines, and some types
of systems that are now on the market can handle sixty-four bits at once.
Remember, to get the number of bytes, you have to divide these numbers by eight (which I refuse to do, as it reminds me too much of fourth
grade). So computers are getting faster and faster. And so far we've been
looking at machines that have a single microprocessor, or chip. But today there are machines on the market that have **multiprocessing** capability because they have more than one chip—as many as twenty, in fact.
Computing problems are split up and assigned to the microprocessor
that has some clear track, so to speak.

Now you have all these trains running crazily along their electronic
tracks carrying their information through the microprocessor. Do they
all follow the same path? Just as with the model railroad, or a real one
for that matter, there are **instruction sets** that provide traffic signals and
directions for the little locomotives. Just as well, too, given the speeds at
which this stuff is going. Remember that light travels at 186,000 miles
per second, which means that's the theoretical speed of our little electronics locomotives. That means that if the journey these little bits and
bytes had to make were 186,000 miles long, our electronic train would
complete its journey in one second.* But the chip is tiny, as we've seen,
so each bit of information gets through its journey in millionths of a
second.

*Ignoring friction and the slower switching speeds encountered along the way.

But never fast enough to satisfy the hardware designers. Originally the instruction sets allowed for every conceivable movement of the electronic train that might possibly be called for by any kind of program. So you got very complex instruction sets to govern what would happen. These were called **CISC,** for complex instruction set computing. The problem was that each little locomotive had to look at the whole instruction set each time it started out, to be sure it didn't miss something important—and that took time.

Then some genius discovered that 80 percent of the work done by computers used only 20 percent of the instruction set. The other 80 percent of the instruction set was used only 20 percent of the time, but it was still there and acted as a drag on the whole system because the locomotive had to waste time reading stuff it would almost never need. So the idea was born of eliminating this 80 percent altogether. You'd give up some functionality, but what you'd get would be a fantastic increase in the speed of the machine.* And so the *RISC* chip was born. This stands for reduced instruction set computing.

Now the trains were really careening down the track! But of course it still wasn't fast enough. All computers have *clocks* inside them, not to tell you when to knock off for lunch, but instead to tell the computer when to release the next set of instructions that'll guide the packets of electrons. For example, a PC might have a 25-**megahertz clock speed.** Now don't panic. *Mega* means "million," and it comes peacefully to us from the Greek for "large." Heinrich Rudolph Hertz was a German physicist who discovered that light comes to us in waves. If your PC runs at 25 MHz, that means that every 25 millionths of a second a new instruction (and in powerful computers more than one instruction) is released to guide those little trains on their way. Of course, computer designers soon discovered that if you could turn up the clock speed, to say, 33 MHz, 40 MHz, or higher, you could squeeze even more blinding speed out of the systems. So that's what they did.

Unfortunately, computer speeds depend on more, ultimately, than just the clock speed. Remember that we're talking about speeds inside the chip. But to get anything to happen, there are other parts of the computer that have to be brought into play, and these too have their effect on speed. For example, you've got other kinds of chips, such as **memory modules,** where information is stored during an operating session, and brought out when it has to be processed. And you've got a special memory hidey hole called a *cache,* which is sort of a temporary storage place not too far from the chip, where your computer puts infor-

---

*A way was also soon found to regain the full functionality of the machine by re-creating complex instructions as composites of the simple instructions.

mation it'll probably need in a hurry; it doesn't want to go all the way back to the memory module to get it.

Your computer also has **input devices** (keyboard, pen, scanners, etc.) and **output devices** (screen, printer, speakers). It also has memory storage (hard disk or floppies or both). Of course it has a **power supply** that takes the 110 volts from the outlet and reduces it to the tiny trickle that computer innards can digest. All these things have to be hooked together, and for this purpose there's a special wiring system called a **bus.** But this isn't just a simple wire. A computer bus takes the electrons and sort of slingshots them along their path whenever the little things show signs of getting tired. In other words, the bus is also very important to the total speed of the computer, and a lot of important advances have been made in this part of the technology.

I can hear you say it: "Why this terrible emphasis on speed? Who gives a darn if an operation takes a few seconds longer?" A lot of problems that computers help us with are extraordinarily complex and just require lots of time to process. If a computer is performing **real-time** control of the emissions of a chemical plant, for example (meaning that it senses and reacts virtually instantly to data it receives), and an explosion is about to occur in .0001 second unless some valve is turned, and there are millions of bits of information being processed each second, then speed becomes critical. Similarly, some problems presented to a computer are so complex that they require the constant manipulation of incredible amounts of information; an example would be composing a color photograph or three-dimensional image on a screen, using a color **scanner** as an input device. That tremendous processing speed also becomes necessary if several programs are running at once, or if many people are using the same computer, connected to it by separate terminals.

Jargon, Technical Terms, and Business Terms

Every industry has its jargon; this is what shows the world that you "belong" in the industry, and what is expressed in jargon can often be expressed in English. Technical terms are a little different; a command of such terms indicates a command of the technology. To be one of the gang, you have to understand the jargon; to advance your learning, you should try to master what lies behind the technical terminology. If you have had no previous exposure to high-tech language, you may be in for a shock. High-tech people look like you and me, but they don't talk like you and me. I asked an artist friend of mine to read and comment on a paragraph from a technical manual put out by the company I work for, Sun Microsystems. Here is the paragraph:

In order to provide an efficient multithreaded kernel, free from deadlocks and starvation, many data structures and algorithms have been redesigned. Hundreds of synchronization locks have been added to the kernel to protect and arbitrate access to critical data structures. These locks use the indivisible test-and-set instructions provided by the . . . architecture. . . . Interrupt levels are no longer used to provide mutual exclusion.*

And here are his comments:

Kernel to me brings the image of Squanto demonstrating to the Pilgrim fathers how to make popcorn. I don't find *deadlocks* in my Webster's, but it has a faintly Caribbean ring. *Starvation* is self-explanatory. I assume that the reference to *data structures and algorithms* is some sort of computerese. But *synchronization locks*? Hundreds of them, added to that poor, inoffensive prepubescent piece of popcorn? Summons up grisly images of the worst offenses of the body-piercing subculture. I like *protect and arbitrate*! Perhaps things are not quite as bad as I thought. And *indivisible*—isn't that what the Pledge of Allegiance says our country is? *Architecture* gives us the comforting thought that above it all some Presence has worked it all out . . . and those nasty interrupt levels are no longer used to mutually exclude people.

It is unlikely that you, as a nontechnical person, will be required to do much better than my friend at deciphering technical literature, at least not initially. But you will not be able to escape the jargon and strange constructs that are used every day by your colleagues at work. There's the story of a young man whom a company hired as a contractor to do administrative work in the engineering department. The first day on the job he overheard a coworker observing that the chief of the department revered UNIX. The young man wore a worried expression for several days until someone explained to him that the reference was to an operating system, not to the guardians of the sultan's harem.

The very best source I've found for explaining technical terms is *The Computer Glossary,* by Alan Freedman.† This is not just a glossary, it's a whole course in high tech disguised as a glossary. If you keep this on

*"Multithreading and Real-Time in Solaris," Copyright 1992, Sun Microsystems, Inc.
†Sixth Edition, AMACOM, New York, 1993.

your desk at home or at work, it will greatly facilitate your self-study. It will help you get a command of the many acronyms that you'll hear every day on the job—a command that most of your colleagues do not have, incidentally. It will describe everything about high tech at the level that you, as a nontechnical person, will require. There are copious illustrations, photos, and diagrams as well. *The Computer Glossary* does not give some of the specialized business terminology, however.

With respect to jargon, I think the best thing to do is to get into it right away. Here's what to look out for as you go in the front door.

Directory of Computer Jargon

access (*vb., trans.*)   To locate, discover: "I can't access your resumé—I know it's got to be around here *somewhere.*"

architect (*vb., trans*)   To plan, to write: "Whoever architected this technical paper really knew his stuff."

beta (*adj.*)   In software, the first version of a new product that is sent out to certain (usually large) customers for testing: "I heard that the beta version is relatively free of bugs."

box (*n.*)   A computer.

bundle (*vb., trans.*)   To include one product with another: "Windows 3.1 came bundled with my PC."

channel (*n.*)   A distributor, VAR (q.v.), OEM (another q.v.), or other reseller acting as an intermediary in moving your products to market: "Sales are down in the Balkans; maybe we should rethink our channels strategy."

configure (*vb., trans.*)   To arrange hardware and software into a usable system; also, to arrange anything into a system: "We've got a space problem here, so when you come in we'll have to reconfigure this broom closet."

CS (*n.*)   Customer service; often includes services such as hotlines, repair, customer training on products, upgrades, and other after-sale activities.

cube (*n.*)   Cubicle; your workspace or office in a company whose spatial philosophy includes the use of low, movable partitions: "Jane's cube is ten inches wider than mine, how did she engineer that?"

datapoint (*n.*)   Fact: "The third datapoint in your cover letter really touches on how we can use your background in psycholinguistics in our PR department."

down (*adj.*)   Not working, not functioning: "The whole network was down for ten hours after the thunderstorm."

downsizing (*n.*)   Layoffs in the industry; also, the move of a customer from larger systems to smaller ones.

drag-and-drop (*vb., trans.*)   Sounding like a dance craze from the forties, this actually refers to manipulating the cursor on the monitor screen so as to move files from one place to another; for example, from a folder to the printer.

end user (*n.*)   The person who actually makes use of a product in his or her daily life.

EOL (*adj.*)   End of life; what happens to a high-tech piece of hardware after a few months, whether customers are still buying it or not. Also used as a verb: "I hear that Product Marketing's gonna EOL the Viper machine next June."

functionality (*n.*)   Usefulness; always preceded by the word *enhance*: "The new multithreading through the kernel to the shell produces enhanced multi-tasking functionality."

geo (*n.*)   Short for *geography*, but used to mean an area or region of the world: "The discounts for the European geo are too high." "She's taken three weeks to tour all the geos and review their CS policies."

goal (*vb., trans.*)   To set a target (for someone); usually used in the past participle form: "Joe was goaled to close three million last quarter."

goodness (*n.*)   That which is desirable: "She postponed the decision on whether to make a hiring offer to Tom, and from the other candidates' point of view that had to be goodness."

GUI (*n.*)   Pronounced "gooey," this stands for Graphical User Interface, the system of little icons and menus on your computer's monitor screen that make the software easier to use.

headcount (*n.*)   An open job backed by actual appropriated money: "You'd be just right for this job. If only I could get a headcount."

icon (*n.*)   The sole contribution of the Russian Orthodox Church to the world of information technology, this expression refers to any one of the little pictures on your computer screen that stand for various operations of the system, thus making the system usable by illiterates.

interface (*vb., intrans.*)   To meet (always followed by *with*): "I guess you've already interfaced with the HR folks, right?"

iron (*n.*)   A computer.

ISV (n.)   Short for Independent Software Vendor. The ISV makes software that actually is useful to the end user, such as spread sheets, word processing programs, tax preparation programs, and many thousands of others.

leverage (*vb., trans.*)   To multiply an effort through the use of intermediaries: "We can leverage our distributors' sales forces to get better coverage of the market."

look and feel (*n.*)   Not an invitation to licentiousness, but the unique nature of a GUI; this is patentable as intellectual property.

map (to) (vb., intrans.)   To correlate with, correspond to: "Your undeniable talents just don't map to our needs at present."

media (*n.*)   The tangible product in which software is contained; therefore, a floppy disk, hard disk, tape, CD, etc. Always used as a singular noun; you will never hear the word *medium* (unless you work in a group of spiritualists).

migrate (*v., trans.*)   To gently nudge a customer from one version of what you're selling to another, sometimes improved version, while garnering more revenue along the way: "We're gonna try to migrate the universities from the Viper DX99 to the Boomslang ZX007, 'cause the Viper's going EOL."

mindshare (*n.*)   Attention: "I've tried to get an additional headcount on my boss's agenda, but I'm competing for mindshare with the new bonus system."

MIPS (*n.*)   Millions of instructions per second; a now out of date way of measuring the speed of a system.

multitask (*v., intrans.*)   To be overcome with work: "I tried to set you up with our marketing manager, but between fighting the reorg, closing out Q1, and working on customer visits, he's multitasking today."

numbers (*n.*)   In sales, the sales goal or target for a salesperson: "Did Jeannie make her numbers last quarter? I haven't seen her around recently."

OEM (*n.*)   Short for Original Equipment Manufacturer. The OEM buys what you make, and tucks it away inside something he makes. The end user isn't aware it's there (unless it breaks).

outplace (*vb., trans.*)   To fire (someone): "Tim and Jane were outplaced last Friday."

penetration (*n.*)   Degree of success in the market with a product. The phallic connotation is intentional, the market being regarded by marketing folks (male and female) as a supine and willing receptacle for whatever new schemes they come up with: "We've had good penetration with our new Zotz CD drive." (This expression is never used by sales reps, who have no time to reflect on such things.)

reorg (*n.*)   Reorganization of a department, division, or company, sometimes synonymous with chaos: "I hear a new reorg is coming down." Occurs frequently.

reprofile (vb., trans.)   To update one's knowledge and skills: "The engineers had to reprofile themselves in a hurry to avoid being outplaced."

req (*n.*)   Often confused with the Arabic word for "petition to the Grand Vizier," it is short for *requisition*, the formal application from the hiring manager to her superiors to approve creation of a job: "Your background in early religions of the Ainu is just what we need for our new marketing campaign; I'm going to put in a req tomorrow."

rightsizing (*n.*)   Used to describe the situation where a potential customer has come to his senses and decided to throw out his costly old mainframe and replace it with your company's systems.

RTU (*n.*)   Right to use; what you get when you buy a software license.

rollout (*n.*)   Introduction of a new product to the marketplace: "They chose the Pago-Pago Hilton for the rollout of the Zaftig-3 server.

SCSI (*adj.*)   Pronounced "scuzzy," this is not an insult. It means Small Computer System Interface. Very few people in the computer industry know this (or indeed the meaning of most acronyms they use), but that doesn't inhibit them from dropping them freely: "The new 90-MHz FlashPlus comes with 8 megs of RAM, 120 megs on the hard drive, a ZQ bus, and 3 scuzzy ports."

SE (*n.*)   Sales engineer. A person who provides invaluable assistance to the sales rep by installing demonstration systems, fixing problems, and answering the tough technical questions posed by the customer's engineers.

spiff (*vb. trans.*)   To offer a monetary incentive to a salesperson: "The district manager spiffed the sales guys $100 for every X30 box they sold last quarter."

support (*vb., trans.*) In high-tech language, this verb means the same thing it means in English, but always used backwards. That is, a high-tech person will say, "the new system supports both the Frammis Plus and Didgery-Doo Operating Systems," making it seems as if the new system is doing the two operating systems some sort of favor, such as making them more salable. In reality, it is the two operating systems that make the computer system worth anything at all to end users—without them, it is an expensive piece of junk.

system (*n.*) The word to use when you want to use the word *computer*. To a high-tech type, the "computer" is a chip somewhere inside a metal box.

timeframe (*n.*) Gratuitous sign of specious erudition added to the name of a month: "I just got a call from my boss—can we reschedule this interview around the September timeframe?"

timeout (*n.*) Sign language signifying that the person using it wishes to override your conversation with the hiring manager to discuss where they should go for lunch. A minor timeout is signaled by making a T with the two forefingers. A major timeout (e.g., where it's already five past twelve) is made with the forearms. (You will not see any of this, since it will be done behind your back—unless you are sitting in the hiring manager's chair and he is sitting with his back to the door.)

twisted pair (*n.*) Not a perverse duo act on MTV, but telephone wires in a building; one of the possible cabling systems for a local area network.

up and running (*adj. phr.*) Working, functioning: "My SE finally got the system up and running."

upgrade (vb., n.) To improve a piece of hardware or software by adding something to it, or by replacing it with an improved version (vb). The latest or improved version (n).

value add (*n.*) Contribution. Often seen in context of a query: "What's his value add to the team?" or, sometimes, pseudo-bravado: "Let's make an extra effort to get some value add on the project."

VAR (*n.*) Short for Value Added Reseller, one of the channels used to get product into the hands of end users.

version (*n.*) In the software world, the latest product, incorporating improvements, bug fixes, or whatever is needed to solve problems that arose in the earlier software. The version of software is indicated by a series of numbers. Thus Windows 3.1 is an improved version of Windows 3.0.

virtual (*adj.*) Characterizing that which isn't really there, but can be called into being when necessary, so we pretend that it is really there all along. Used for everything in the high-tech industry and in the lives of its denizens; impossible to misuse, since no one really understands it: "You never see Jenny with Tom; she's his virtual girlfriend." "I had a virtual pizza for lunch." "All I have in my purse is virtual money."

wysiwyg (*adj.*) Neither a Dickens character nor the Latvian Minister for Home Affairs, this acronym stands for What You See Is What You Get—i.e., what is on the computer screen is exactly what will print out.

5

The Culture of the High-Tech Company

Companies have cultures, just as do nations, tribes, and ethnic groups. And it's important that you understand your company's culture. To put it bluntly, if you are not at ease with the culture of your high-tech company, at best you will be unhappy, and at worst you may find yourself out the door. A woman who came to the industry from several years in retail sales observed:

> I think that the culture, learning about that before you pick a job, is probably the most critical factor that is going to allow you to stay in that particular company for any length of time.

You therefore owe it to yourself to learn as much as you can about a company's culture before you join up. Why is this notion of "culture" so important in the workplace? Because a company is really like a community, with its own set of values, its own ethos, and its own written and unwritten codes of behavior. Companies, of course, unlike most communities, are intentionally organized to attain certain goals, the most important of which are to generate revenues and produce profits. But companies do not pursue business in value-neutral ways. Company values are the foundation on which the corporate culture rests.

This chapter takes a look at value statements, then goes on to consider five aspects of the high-tech culture. These are:

1. Informality and egalitarianism
2. Management styles
3. Emphasis on learning and relearning
4. Responsibility for career development and security
5. Styles of communication

The chapter then briefly looks at the benefits that go along with a high-tech job, and closes by addressing the notion of the "culture of credibility."

Value Statements

You should not be so desperate to be employed that you do not expend some effort on finding out what the corporate values of your potential employer are. Top executives in most companies in the high-tech industry and in many other industries spend time thinking about values and often express them in a corporate "mission statement" or other written document.* In Motorola, each of the company's 100,000 employees carries a copy of the company's mission statement on a wallet-size card.

You might be tempted to scoff at the idea of profit-driven senior managers devoting significant amounts of time to such a pursuit, and in any case you may well ask what happens to such high-flown sentiments by the time they percolate down to where they really might have an impact on the environment you will be working in. In fact, although in some older industries there seems to be less impact on middle management, in the high-tech industry, statements of the company's mission and values really do affect the way business is done. One of the reasons for this is that employees at all levels may participate in defining the company's mission. Also, high-tech corporations tend to be fairly young, and have tended to adopt and maintain the values held dear by the founders, who are often still actively involved as top executives or directors. Another reason is that high-tech industry prides itself on representing what is best in American business: Using the country's best brains to innovate in the areas of product development and marketing and thus maintain world technological leadership. This perception leads those at the helm to be both hardheaded business people and idealists, and they wish their companies to reflect their idealism in all aspects of the business. This is why one finds such themes in high-tech corporate mission statements as honesty, treating the customer right, treating employees with respect, etc.

Not all value statements are expressed in writing. National Semiconductor, whose managers and employees have done an astounding job of turning the company around financially, growing the business,

*An exception to this is IBM; its president, Louis Gerstner, said in mid-1993 that "the last thing IBM needs now [i.e., as the company tries to recover from devastating losses) is a vision." Gerstner seems to think that he can solve IBM's problems without engaging the hearts and minds of tens of thousands of employees; time will tell whether he is correct.

and adding value to its products, has done things differently. A young woman who works at National told me:

> We know that we have to go through a huge transformation here in order to become the kind of company that will survive in the high technology of the future in the semiconductor industry. And so we've done this very bizarre thing, and its probably one of the reasons I like working here so well. We've done a vision, and it's done graphically . . . and part of this visioning process that National is going through is to change our whole image and to change our orientation to become a more people-oriented company. . . . We're actually going through what's called a redesign, looking at our company from a systems point of view. . . . It's all driven by shared values.
>
> I would say that at this point [we've involved] about 2,000 managers; we've gone down through the levels in the corporation, and we'll go through all 26,000 people expressing what this vision is, and having them have an input into how they want to change it.

The time to find out about company values is when you think you've identified an employment opportunity. But how do you go about finding out what these values are? You can write to the company's vice-president for human resources and ask for a mission statement, but you probably won't get an answer. If you're interviewing in a company, you can ask any HR person to get you a copy. But since I advise you to steer clear of the HR department for as long as possible, the best way is simply to ask one or two employees in the department you're interested in joining. Managers and individual contributors may joke about corporate values, but they almost always are aware of them.

Value statements are sometimes made orally. For example, Sun Microsystems' president, Scott McNealy, has told employees on many informal occasions to "walk away" from doubtful business. In other words, give up a potential sale if any step toward that sale would involve any unethical action. McNealy says that the company's reputation for honesty and proper business practices cannot be jeopardized for any reason. Similarly, during the years I was at Digital Equipment Corporation, there was a saying that used to surface from time to time; I am sure that every employee of the company had at least heard it once: "If you don't know what to do, do what is right."

Sometimes divisions or departments of high-tech companies will develop their own value statements. Elise, a young woman who worked in the financial department of a hardware company, had participated in this process:

> I had a few small projects, and one of them was writing a statement of our department's values and goals. There are, I think, nine values. I should have memorized them by now, but I haven't. But I remember generally. Appreciation for cross-cultural values. Respect for individuals. Integrity, being professional. These things are what we value. We wanted to get the word out to the whole group that these are our values.

There is no question but that value statements like these have appeal to employees. They provide business with a sort of moral structure, and indicate that companies where they are current are probably good places to work. Strange as it may seem, these statements do seem to inform the day-to-day actions and utterances of many middle-level managers and individual contributors in the high-tech industry. Perhaps this is a result of a self-selection process. People who don't have respect for cross-cultural values, for example, probably sense that they wouldn't feel comfortable working in an environment where ethnocentrism is simply regarded as irrelevant, so these sorts of people just don't join up. Or perhaps value statements do have some kind of influence on people's behavior.

Whatever the reason, these sorts of statements form the underpinning of the company's culture, which in turn touches every aspect of the high-tech working day. The way people talk to each other, dress, interact, conduct meetings, reward extra effort, play are all informed by the culture. It has influenced the design of the building you walk into every morning, the office layout, and the various services provided. It affects company policies and the way the company communicates these to the employees. And it's what employees usually turn to when you ask them, "What's it like working at . . . ?"

What Makes High-Tech Culture Unique

There are five factors that make the high-tech industry's culture unique.

Informality and Egalitarianism

Elsewhere I've mentioned that race, ethnic and social background, gender, and formal education matter less in high tech than they do in other industries. The same can be said for the hierarchy within the high-tech industry itself. My first exposure to the egalitarian nature of the culture in high tech involved getting used to using first names only, regardless of rank. When Kenneth Olsen was the CEO of Digital Equipment Corporation, everyone referred to him as "Ken." A good many of these people had never met or even seen him in person, yet each felt that he or she had a personal link with him. And this is generally true throughout the high-tech industry. The informality tends to blur the distinction between commoners and kings in a way that does not exist in many traditional corporations.

One of the most striking aspects of Digital Equipment Corporation's egalitarian culture is the layout of its offices. Visitors to the company notice that, with a few exceptions, there are no closed offices at DEC. But the interesting thing is that the few closed offices that do exist are all inside offices; that is, they have no windows. The story behind this has become a part of DEC's culture. Many years ago, the story goes, Ken Olsen was being shown around a new building. The facilities manager showed him where the majority of employees would sit—in interior cubicles. Then the tour leader proudly pointed out the managers' closed offices, each with a window wall looking out over the beautiful New England countryside. After the tour was over, Olsen was asked how he liked the building. "It's fine," he said, "but there's been a mistake." The bewildered manager asked him what was wrong. "You've got the managers sitting where the employees are going to sit," said Olsen. "In this company the employees have the windows." The building was reconfigured, and from that day on no manager ever occupied an office with a window.

Is that a true story? It hardly matters (though it is true that managers' offices at DEC don't have windows, for whatever reason). The point is that DEC's employees believed it was true. They knew Ken Olsen was looking out for their interests.

In some industries the top managers not only have luxurious offices, they also have special dining rooms and park in choice reserved parking areas. Though some of that hangs on in the older segments of the high-tech industry, notably in some semiconductor companies, in most companies executives eat at the same facilities as the troops and trudge in from the same remote parking lots.

Various companies in the high-tech industry have different approaches to dress codes, but in general dress is much less formal than in other industries. A young man told me:

> Well, in [former employer] wearing a blue shirt was very important. Blue shirt, red tie. The role in that business was, as

a corporate staffer, to convey the corporate image. That was more important than you as a person. More important than who you were, what you said, how you acted was the fact of what you represented. That's why the suit was so important. It represented a sort of stability, a corporate image. A solidity. And frankly, an intolerance for nonconformity. . . . Conveying the established corporate rules and policies was more important than being creative individually.

One can generalize about this and say that the old-line companies are more formal, in that they have fairly rigid ideas on how people should dress, the length of their hair, and so forth, whereas the younger companies are less formal. People in the high-tech industry who meet customers usually have to dress up more than those who lurk in the cubicles. But there are lots of variants on this theme. It's a commonplace in the industry that software engineers, for example, are as informal in appearance as their minds are orderly. They usually don't meet customers—that is, they don't go out and sell—but sometimes their presence is required during a customer visit. A Silicon Valley firm was once hosting an important potential customer from the Far East. This gentleman was

Dress in the high-tech industry is less formal.

courted by a series of attentive young sales and marketing reps in power suits. When the time came for the presentation from the software folks, the door opened and three of the scruffiest individuals imaginable entered the room. These were the software geniuses, to whom everyone deferred, including the visitor from Asia.

Most new employees who come from old-line industries find this informality refreshing. I spoke to a young woman who came from an old-line large consumer products company to work in a successful computer company in California, which we'll call Datadrive:

> And I'll tell you, my first introduction to Datadrive was just, I was just . . . so disgusted! I could not believe that grownup people behaved this way! [*Laughs.*] First of all, I'm coming from [her former employer], where people walk around in dark jackets. This is, you know, we know how to behave! And you know, I'm also a Southerner, and we have sort of codes for the way people are supposed to treat each other, and that was a big transition for me, just living in a different state where things are just a lot different. Much more liberal. And so I'm making that transition at the same time I'm coming in, and here's all these people wearing Birkenstocks and jeans! And I was like, don't you have any respect? [*Laughs.*] I was really up tight.

Scott McNealy of Sun Microsystems commented on his company's culture in this way:

> Sun Microsystems has been a very diverse environment. The computer industry has always been diverse. For example, I don't care what jewelry you wear, or where. And the only dress code at Sun is that you must. It just doesn't matter. . . . I have a saying at Sun: have lunch or be lunch. The only thing that matters is output. . . . you've got to do that while getting along with everyone and being part of the team.

Management Styles

There is almost no traditional middle management in the high-tech industry, in the sense of directing and controlling of subordinates, and so individuals have considerable autonomy in how they structure and perform their jobs. People may be told about problems and then left to solve them. More likely they are not even told about problems; they are just asked to go to work and report periodically on what is happening. They can seek advice from whomever they can find to help them. There is also little week-to-week monitoring of performance, though there is a formal "performance review," in some companies every six months, and in some every year. Setting of goals and monitoring of performance will become more difficult for high-tech managers in the future as the industry moves to a flatter configuration, with perhaps as many as forty to sixty individual contributors reporting to a single manager. The manager's job will be to participate with the individual employees in working out goals, to advise the people reporting to him or her, and to facilitate their performance, but there will be no time for looking over people's shoulders.

Not all high-tech companies are moving toward this view of management at the same speed, however, and some of them, notably the old-line semiconductor companies that had styles verging on the militaristic, have farther to go. Here is what one woman had to say about her former employer:

> I don't know if all the semiconductor companies are like this, but I can bet they are. . . . It's kind of a management by fear. The culture is management by fear—who can yell louder. If you can yell, you're respected. It was just a bunch of b___s___, and I don't believe in doing business like that. I don't believe in intimidating people to do what you want to do. My philosophy of life doesn't fit into that.

And another woman in a semiconductor company had some difficulties trying to get across to her manager a point that concerned hiring new employees:

> He got up in my face, he was like screaming, spitting, bright red in the face, telling me how dare I tell him that we didn't really look at their skill sets . . . he was screaming at me. And I don't like that. I told him he was a f_____ a_____ and I walked out. A corporate VP called me for that and was screaming at me on the phone and I hung up on him. And you know, after that my job became very easy. People thought I was great! And I thought this was the stupidest place I've worked at in my whole life!
>
> I think that's how the [semiconductor] industry got started. It's been watered down, but still. . . ."

But this segment of the high-tech industry is also changing, driven by competitive pressures. Earlier I mentioned National Semiconductor's efforts to change its culture. A man who has worked there for several years observed:

> We were known as the animals of Silicon Valley. Very aggressive. The orientation was, get it done right now and produce a lot very quickly. There wasn't an orientation toward quality. It was a driver culture, where what's important is that you get results and get them quickly. Then you have cultures that are more people-oriented; the whole orientation is based around making sure the people are happy and in a happy environment. They are also productive, but the focus is on the people.
>
> Part of the process we're going through now is to become more people-oriented. Because it had gone so far the other way that people weren't very happy here, and they were losing a lot of good people for that reason. . . . We're taking a look at where we came from, what was valuable and we want to retain, and what we want to become in the future.

Another way cultures can change is if a company is purchased by a larger company with a different culture. A few years ago IBM bought a small company called Rolm, which was in the telecommunications industry. It's generally conceded that this acquisition was a disaster for Rolm and an unhappy event in the history of IBM; the companies eventually parted ways. Here's how an employee who was working for Rolm described the situation:

> I came to the conclusion that this was not a place I wanted to work, because as IBM purchased the company, the culture changed. You had IBM, a conservative company, coming into a startup high-tech young company, and the clash was unbelievable. There was a lot of pain, a lot of blood so to speak, trying to mix the management and the staff. And I realized very quickly that sales were dropping. I don't know whether they dropped because IBM bought it and the company rebelled, or whether the owners of Rolm realized this would happen and sold out right before it hit.

Management style also includes trusting the people who work for you. Sun Microsystems, for example, has no procedure to track vacation time taken by its exempt employees. Nor does anyone care what time you come to work. It's all done on trust. The result is that the parking lots start to fill up before eight in the morning and are still filled at six in the evening. Contrast this with the following statement from a person who interviewed with Digital Equipment Corporation:

> I interviewed with DEC once and wouldn't take the job because the manager said, 'Well you really do have to be in at 9:00 A.M.' And there are other places I wouldn't consider working because they paid attention to hours. With Data General and with Sun that was just not a concern. They expect people to be professionals and in fact overwork themselves.

And a young man who interviewed for a job with Cabletron told me:

> The hiring manager said I'd be expected to be in by eight and to work until five. These are the official hours.

(He decided to accept the job.)

Authoritarian managers are already rarities in most of the industry, and in a few years either they will disappear or the companies that tolerate them will disappear. Management styles that encourage risk-taking and independence on the part of employees will be the norm because they will fit in best with the developing reliance on strong, confident, and able individual contributors. As one woman who is a technical writer in a hardware company told me:

> I'm starting to be of the opinion that you find the right boss or you make the boss you have be the right boss. . . . The second boss I had here was a real knockout. I was empowered; I was encouraged to grow and to take risks. And my goodness, from the humble technical writer who arrived here and wrote a bunch of board installations, I was managing all kinds of stuff and doing all kinds of stuff. . . . [Managers now] say, "find a need and fill it!" And there are all kinds of needs right now.

Emphasis on Training and Retraining

At Apple, for example, there are several training organizations that offer function-specific training. In all there are about 150 staff persons involved in training in the company; there is also extensive use of contractors and consultants. Apple University is a training organization with a more general mission. It was established as a means of communicating the company's business direction, improving management skills, and increasing the effectiveness of the individual contributor. Both courses and the "BIZ" series of management modules are offered in these areas. What distinguishes them from courses in an academic environment is that they are short (½ to 3 days) and highly focused on a particular problem. Management modules offered in early 1994 included the following from the Apple University curriculum:*

Leadership Approaches to Decision Making

This module will help managers understand their own decision making approach in groups. Managers will learn when other approaches are appropriate and how to move decisions to implementation.

Giving Effective Feedback

Using a simple planning model, managers will be asked to practice giving feedback based on a case and one situation they have had or are going to deal with. The majority of the time will be spent on difficult feedback, with some time practicing positive feedback.

Planning and Running Effective Meetings

This module focuses on two areas: meeting management and facilitating difficult behavior [sic]. Managers will be asked to practice their facilitation skills and plan for an upcoming meeting using the tools discussed in the program.

Managers' Role in Team Building

Using the Team Effectiveness Profile, managers will assess their team's performance in five areas—planning, organizational structure, processes, and interpersonal and intergroup relations. Managers will receive coaching on how to increase effectiveness in one key area and develop an action plan.

Other management modules are available on videotape.
 An example of a three-day course at Apple University is:

*These course descriptions are used with the kind permission of Apple University.

So . . . You Wanna Manage

Target audience: Individual contributors . . . who have been identified by their manager as potential candidates for promotion to a management position within the next 6–12 months.

Purpose: So . . . You Wanna Manage is a three-day workshop designed to help participants: (1) understand basic components of effective management; and (2) determine if they want to pursue a management position.

Learning Objectives: At the conclusion of this course, participants will be able to:

- Understand the impact of interpersonal styles on managing
- Delegate tasks effectively
- Set clear performance expectations
- Give specific performance feedback
- Increase their capacity to listen and communicate effectively

Career Self-Reliance

Employees are responsible for staying employed and for managing their own career development. Again, the situation at Apple is indicative of what is happening in most of the larger high-tech companies. Apple has recently established a new service, the Career Resource Center, "to provide career management services and partnerships that support the convergent needs of employees and Apple; and empower employees to . . . manage their careers, commit to life-long learning, and make informed choices in a changing world of work." One element of its mission is to provide "support and service to employees transitioning within and outside of Apple." As Betsy Collard, of the Palo Alto Career Action Center in Silicon Valley and an authority on career development, puts it, career self-reliance is "the ability to actively manage your worklife in a rapidly changing environment. [It's] the attitude of being self-employed whether you are in or outside an organization."*

This emphasis on managing one's own fate is very different from the way the industry started out. In its early years, and probably right up to 1991, companies created an atmosphere of nurturance of their em-

*From "Creating a Career Resilient Workforce," a presentation given June 29, 1993.

ployees. *Nurturance* is a general term encompassing all the attitudes and policies that are intended to recognize the great, even unique value of each employee to the company, and the regard in which top management holds him or her. The statement "our employees are our greatest asset" implies that we will nurture, care for, and develop our employees, and in exchange we know they will give their best efforts toward achieving our goals. Virtually every new high-tech company started operations with nurturance as an important element of its culture, and as long as the company did well, the system worked and inspired fanatical devotion.

A senior manager at IBM, a company well known for its paternalism toward its employees, said:

> When you came into IBM, money wasn't so important. I used to say to people I was interviewing that if they wanted to come here for money, they would leave for money. Our pay by itself was not competitive in the marketplace. The assumption was you're getting other things out of this job. Working with really smart people. Being part of the leadership in the industry. Being able to say you worked for IBM!

Imagine the fantastic loyalty involved in being part of IBM in those good old days, where one could take pride in being paid less than the market rate!

One important aspect of the culture of large companies in the high-tech industry today is the switch from the nurturance environment to the adult environment. This change is driven by economic pressures in both the hardware and software parts of the business. Many of these pressures come from overseas; in India, for example, an excellent software programmer can be hired for $700 per month compared with perhaps $5,000 per month in the United States. On the hardware side, there are more and more companies getting into the business, both in this country and in low-cost "clone-maker" countries such as Taiwan and Korea, so profit margins are being driven ever lower.

In addition, the industry has matured to a degree undreamed of in the days of young inventors creating products in a garage. As Scott McNealy of Sun Microsystems says:

> Performance becomes very, very clear. It didn't used to, in the 1970s and 1980s. There were a lot of incompetent managers. It was kind of like being in real estate in California in the 1960s. Bozo the Clown became a billionaire. But all of a sudden now you find out who the good real estate people are

and who are the smart ones. That's true in the computer industry. It's still a big, huge, fast-growing business, but it's no longer one for amateurs, for part-timers, or for accidental millionaires. You earn it. Nobody will ever do another deal like IBM did for Bill Gates. That isn't going to happen. Those mistakes have all been made, and we're into the big leagues now.

The technology, too, is changing so rapidly that people who have spent years acquiring a technical education and skills find the ground slipping out from under them. As a senior manager told me:

The fundamental concept is that the particular tactical skill that is needed for the next eighteen months will change in the next eighteen months.

This, plus the fact that companies are now bluntly informing employees that they own responsibility for their own careers, is putting incredible pressure on engineers to upgrade and change their skills. The same manager went on to say:

If that person wants to stay on the leading edge of technology, he continually has to reeducate himself. In this company the vice-presidents in charge of development have said they have to reeducate the entire workforce every four years. . . . Right now, facing [a change in software technology], it's as if we're teaching everybody to play the violin the other way around—from bowing with the right hand to bowing with the left hand. Or for a writer, maybe it's as if we'd changed all the rules of grammar.

But upgrading skills is not such an easy thing to do. One problem is knowing which knowledge is becoming obsolete, then figuring out what new knowledge has to be acquired to take its place. Managers are supposed to assist engineers in working this out, but they, too, find it difficult to divine where the technology gods want them to go. The impact on company culture arises from the stresses associated with this change, which are beginning to produce intense unhappiness in some of the engineering community. Having led the high-tech charge for so many years, having in a sense actually defined the industry, these men and women suddenly find themselves vulnerable. For the first time their careers seem to be at risk for reasons that have nothing to do with their performance, but rather with the rapid change in technology itself.

Paradoxically, the high-tech employees who find themselves the least affected by such pressures, and whose relative position in the industry is growing stronger, are the people whose basic skill sets are nontechnical, but who understand the technology sufficiently to use their skills effectively within the industry. In other words, people like you and me.

Communication Methods

Communication in the high tech company is quite different from that in other, more sedate industries. It's important for you to get a rapid fix on how employees communicate ideas to one another, to customers and suppliers, and especially upwards. In college you learned the importance of writing clearly, of organizing your thoughts concisely on paper, of structuring your arguments so as to withstand close scrutiny. In the high-tech industry this generally does not apply to any internal communications. The most important high-tech internal communications are verbal. The least important are written. The reason for this is simple: People believe they do not have the time to read and digest a memo. Writing is important in the following areas:

- *Legal*—contracts, memoranda and the like
- *PR*—press releases
- *Technical*—manuals, technical papers
- *Human Resources*—employee evaluations, etc.

It is not significantly important in any other area. Business letters are virtually obsolete, having been replaced by the fax, the phone, and E-mail. But the *skills* involved in being able to write well are critical to another means of communication in the high-tech industry, the *presentation*, which is an important part of the high-tech culture.

Applicants for positions in the high-tech industry are often asked whether they have experience in making presentations. The reason is that often your ideas will have to be communicated upwards to senior management. Usually they will be communicated by your standing up in front of a meeting, using a whiteboard, overheads (i.e., transparencies), or slides, and having five to ten minutes to get your ideas across. The same applies to ideas you want to share with your manager or your colleagues: You will almost invariably find yourself standing at the whiteboard writing your ideas down in abbreviated form as you talk. This is why all offices in the high-tech industry come with whiteboards on the walls; even impromptu "drop-in" meetings usually end up with someone scribbling something down.

Though many high-tech companies offer courses on how to give an effective presentation, the quality of most presentations is abysmal. This is surprising, given that being able to present well is often an important determinant in getting recognition and promotions. In Chapter 6 you'll find a few simple rules for putting on a good presentation.

When you deal with the written word in a high-tech setting, you will use E-mail, which gives everyone in the company the ability to communicate in writing, and increasingly with the addition of voice and pictures, with any other employee, from the president to the sales manager in Australia. And through external networks, such as Internet, you will be able to send messages almost instantly to people or groups throughout the world. This actually puts extraordinary power into the hands of each employee and represents quite an expression of faith on the part of top management. The universal availability of E-mail communications is a stunning democratic technological feat. Being in daily contact with sales reps in Sweden and Singapore, or customer service managers in Boston and Budapest strengthens the feeling of belonging to a big family within the company.

As you begin to use this technology, you may be tempted to write rather coherent, well-structured E-mail memos any time you have something important to say. Save your energy. If your memos are longer than three brief paragraphs, no one will read them, and you will get a reputation for verbosity. Here's what one bemused new hire had to say about internal electronic mail in his company:

> One thing that killed me was E-mail. Like at [former employer], I was used to writing memos and having them read two or three times before I even sent them to my boss. You know, I just wanted to make sure that . . . I would read them and have my peers read them, we would edit each other's work and stuff to make sure it was perfect, it looked nice, you'd spend all this time on the word processor. Before I'd send a note to my boss! Because people would *evaluate* you on that kind of stuff, on how it looked. That was very important.
>
> And then here I'd get these E-mails and they're like misspelled, there's no punctuation, they're writing all over the page . . . and I'm going, Who wrote this? Does anybody care? [*Laughs*].
>
> You know, I was just shocked. And it was just a huge transition for me. I have loosened up a lot. I'm a lot less tight than I was.

In some companies memos and even E-mails are considered too time-consuming. In one of the fastest-growing companies in California, a young channels manager observed:

> Here the most important means of communication is voice-mail. It's amazing. There's a whole culture around voicemail. And meetings. We have tons of meetings. The voicemail types of commitments are about 70 percent commitments. A face-to-face meeting commitment is about 90 percent. I don't know if you ever get a 100 percent commitment, just because things change rapidly. So the commitment you made yester-day might be OK but not applicable today. Maybe a 100 per-cent commitment would be getting a req signed off so you could hire someone. But again, if you don't hire someone right away, there's no guarantee they won't pull that thing right back the next day.

Salaries and Benefits in the High-Tech Industry

Salaries

What do all these jobs pay? It's not possible to be specific, because there are so many variables. Salary standards and the cost of living vary from one part of the country to another. For each position in the high-tech industry, there is always a *salary range,* and there is often a huge differ-ence between the lowest pay and the highest for any given job. Also, companies have different compensation philosophies; some make it a point to pay at the top end, while others are content to rest in the top quarter or top half of what the industry is paying. Obviously there are some companies that pay in the bottom 25 percent. Unless such a com-pany is a startup and is willing to give you stock options, it's probably not a good idea to start out there.

Suffice it to say that the high-tech industry in general pays very well, better for a given level of experience than any other I know of. And there are usually unparalleled opportunities to continue one's education at company expense, both in formal degree programs and by taking courses within the company, which I count as nontaxable income. And, finally, the mobility within the industry, where a receptionist can be-come a marketing manager and a PR writer can move into sales, is an-other untaxed benefit. I'm not sure how or whether this can be quanti-fied, but I suspect it's worth a lot to most high-tech employees.

Benefits

The nurturance culture in high tech has generally resulted in good benefits. These usually include excellent health insurance; in the larger companies access to internal training and development courses, higher education courses, and degree programs at colleges and universities at company expense; and employee stock purchase and 401(k) retirement plans. Some companies also offer stock option plans to all employees, not just to top executives, though this is not the norm. A few high-tech companies, such as Apple, give employees "sabbaticals"—extra weeks of vacation every few years. These benefits can easily add up to 30 percent of your basic salary, and companies are starting to take a long, hard look at benefit plans as they try to chop expenses. The most rapidly rising cost has been health care plans, and most high-tech employers are moving to cap their exposure by requiring employees to assume a greater share of the cost and by inducing them to enroll in health maintenance organizations.

One area where the nurturance culture is not strongly manifested is that of vacation time. Compared to European companies, American firms are notoriously parsimonious when it comes to vacations. You can typically look forward to two weeks of vacation during your first three years on the job, followed by three weeks each year thereafter until you've been on board for eight years. At this point, your vacation will probably increase to four weeks. One problem is that there is a high degree of mobility between companies, and it is very possible that you will not be with the same company for as long as eight years. Whatever new company you move to, you will normally start all over again on the vacation ladder—two weeks is all you'll get for the first three years. European firms (and European subsidiaries and offices of U.S. companies) are generally required to start employees at five weeks' vacation the first year, with additional "comp time" for overtime. Even managers receive additional vacation days for overtime, which is usually defined as any time spent on the job over thirty-seven hours per week!

When you are negotiating for a new position, it is possible to make an informal arrangement with your manager and add a week or two to the vacation time you'd normally get. But if your manager should leave for a new position a few weeks later, all bets are off. There's no guarantee that the new manager will honor the old agreement.

The Culture of Credibility

When you join your colleagues on your first day at work in high tech, very few people will know who you are. Even those participated in in-

terviewing you prior to your being hired, and who have read your resumé, will not really know much about you, except for one or two high
spots on your resumé and the impressions gleaned during the interview. And while you will be given all the friendly support you require
during the early days, you are really undergoing a sort of apprenticeship
until you establish your credibility. Credibility means that people listen
when you speak. It means you get noticed by people who count. It is
really a prerequisite for being fully effective on the job. A woman who
recently joined a rapidly expanding computer company observed:

> There's definitely a culture of how you get things done. Some
> cultures are very much empowerment, go and do it; you have
> a lot of leeway on your own to do it. Others say you have that,
> but in fact you have to work a certain channel of approval in
> order to get things done.
>
> Also how you go about getting credibility to do things. It's
> subtle, but without it you're dead. In some companies you
> could hit one ball, and hit it well, and automatically that
> makes you a hero. In others you have to do that again and
> again and again before you can earn that same stripe. So I
> guess maybe it's a question of where is the bar. In some com-
> panies it's lower, in some it's higher. And there isn't just suc-
> ceeding in the job, there's also succeeding in the relationships
> with people in the company.

High-tech companies generally do not accord much credibility to
activities that do not affect the bottom line. If you are asked to perform
some "good citizen" task that might win you kudos in a traditional old-
line company, you should not expect it to do much to establish your
credibility. A young woman who joined a high-tech manufacturer from
outside the industry found this out after her boss asked her to join a task
force that didn't contribute to the bottom line:

> I would show up at meetings and I would be the only person
> there. And I just was *shocked* that people would behave like
> this. I mean, this is the CFO telling us to do something! First
> of all I saw it as a development opportunity, I saw it as an
> exposure opportunity. I mean at [her former employer], peo-
> ple *killed* for those kinds of things, I mean special task forces,
> Oh My God! The visibility and stuff. And I guess it's a bigger
> company, and older, and it's a lot harder to get your name
> out. People killed for those kinds of opportunities. It was in-

conceivable to me that people would not show up. And also, it was really rude.

I'd be there for fifteen minutes, and finally somebody would roll in and we'd start talking, and we never had an agenda, we never did blah blah blah [*she drawls*], it was all so relaxed, and I just got totally frustrated. I finally ended up doing 80 percent of the project myself. And that was OK, but I didn't really want my personal stamp on this thing. It was supposed to have been a team. That was kind of when I first started understanding that things at [the high-tech company] are very, very relaxed! And that those sorts of codes don't really exist. I mean, you can do your own thing no matter what. And that was reiterated through people's behavior in my own department.

The Final Word on Culture

For most people, becoming immersed in the high-tech culture for the first time is like jumping into a New England lake on a hot day—a shock, followed by delight once you get used to it. Occasionally, though, it's difficult for a person to adjust. At times managers from other companies have tried to impose a different culture on their particular departments. This is usually futile, as many high-tech employees simply won't put up with it. But for the most part problems arise when a a high-tech employee, for one reason or another, takes a job in another industry. The spouse of a woman working in high tech received his MBA from Stanford University a couple of years ago. Failing to find a job in the San Francisco area, the husband returned with his wife to the Midwest. About a year later she returned to Silicon Valley to visit friends. She said:

It's incredible! They [the new employer] are so out of it. Everyone is judged not on performance but how she looks, how she dresses, how much she gets involved in the local church. And they never just rear back and let go! High tech is crazy . . . but I sure miss it!

6

Thriving and Surviving

Once you've landed your job in high tech, you'll discover that a totally new existence has begun for you, at least so far as working is concerned. This chapter covers five important characteristics of your new work environment that will help you flourish and get more out of your work experience. They are establishing credibility by growing the job, getting visibility through presentations, using mentors, making lateral transfers, and continuing your education. The chapter then looks at what you must do to ensure your long-term survival in the high-tech industry. These are rough economic times, and the newspapers are full of stories about employees being laid off. Yet it is possible to avoid this fate by being astute, and by taking preventive measures that will not only assure that you remain employed but increase your value as an employee.

A phrase you'll often hear within the high-tech industry is "growing a job." To grow your job means going beyond the job as it was described to you when you were hired. It also means acquiring new skills and knowledge that permit you to do your job faster and better, and to be on the cutting edge of whatever field you're in, whether it's technical writing, public relations, marketing, or whatever. And it means gaining visibility for yourself and establishing credibility with your coworkers and your managers. The most useful tool for this is the effective presentation.

Growing Your Job

The high-tech industry is very different from other industries in that pushing the boundaries of your job outwards is at worst tolerated and at best strongly encouraged by managers. In many old-line companies, any effort to increase the scope of one's job may be met with suspicion and hostility; the entrepreneurial employee may be figuratively slapped down and told to keep his or her nose to the grindstone and do what he or she is being paid to do. A young woman who is an auditor in a hardware company observed:

> My experience with [former employer] was, I'd go down to Florida, and these guys had been working in these plants for thirty years, where they get a Rolex after so many years. They had two Rolexes! And they're saying, here comes this little girl fresh out of college trying to tell me how to do my job. So I had sort of built up this persona for myself, the way I dress, the way I behave, and that gave me some sort of credibility.
>
> But here [in the high-tech company] that doesn't cut it. You've got to have good ideas, you've got to be articulate, you've got to be able to give presentations, and it doesn't matter what you look like. Which is freeing, but it makes life a lot harder. I mean, you have to work for your credibility a lot more, I think. And coming from Corporate doesn't mean a hell of a lot to people. They could spit and say, 'Who's Corporate? Who cares?' So individual credibility is something you really have to work at.

The following remarks by a high-tech marketing manager also demonstrate the different environment of the high-tech industry, and serve as a neat summary of some of the reasons why it's important to grow your job:

> I find that if you are a nose-to-the-grindstone person who just goes and makes change, that's all you do. People give you a dollar and you give them four quarters. If you do that well, then five years from now that's all you're going to be doing. You're still going to be making change because you're Bob, who makes good change. And your job is not secure. If you're not constantly pushing the mobility barrier, no one's going to push it for you. If you're just sitting in your cube and doing your thing . . . then you have a tendency to be pigeonholed.

There's a lot implicit in this statement, and maybe the most important thing is the notion that you, and you alone, are responsible for your own career development. In fact, growing your job is the first step you'll take toward developing a broader range of skills and abilities in the high-tech industry. Some industry pundit went so far as to observe that the very notion of "job" is disappearing in this country, with the high-tech industry leading the way. This is sometimes referred to as the "dejobbing" of America; what we have are people with sets of skills, who operate sometimes singly but more usually in teams to solve problems and advance the goals of the business. It certainly appears that jobs with well-defined boundaries are becoming an endangered species. The implication for those employees who sit still with their nose to the grindstone is that the job may well move out from under them. So growing your job is often related to long-term survival. There's also the idea that doing the same old thing stereotypes you, and after a while that stereotyping makes it more difficult for you to make a strategic move when you finally decide that's what you want to do. And there is the idea that doing the same job for too long is boring, and makes you a boring person.

But growing your job is also important for more pleasant reasons. In doing so, you meet new people and acquire new knowledge. And you lay the groundwork for lateral moves into areas that you may find more interesting than what you are currently doing. Growing the job also means standing out from the crowd; getting noticed is an absolute prerequisite to getting healthy raises, promotions, or both. A woman who manages several people in a training department told me:

> To establish credibility, you have to get involved in a lot of projects, and that's mostly for visibility. And I think as you gain visibility and you start making presentations and interacting with people in meetings, then your credibility starts to build. It's six months to a year before it starts to build. It's not something that occurs in the first three months, because [the high-tech company she works for] is so different from [traditional companies.]

A man who was graduated about ten years ago with a B.A. in political science and who is now a product manager for a software company said:

> I started off just taking a little project, getting to know the ropes around the company, doing whatever I could just to make this little project successful. Then I started to take on more and more projects, and as I did, I found that you start to meet more people, get more visibility, and people start associating your name with certain products. You go after the opportunities, and if you see something that needs to be addressed, you do it!

That last line probably sums up as well as anything *how* you go about growing your job. Once you've become familiar with your basic tasks and start doing those well, you look around for what needs doing and start doing it. When to inform your manager about your new responsibilities depends on the type of manager she is. A general rule of thumb is to do this early on, either in a one-on-one meeting or in a meeting of your workgroup or department. One thing is certain: Your manager will want to be sure that you are still successfully accomplishing the basic tasks that you two discussed when you first started out. These are the ones that are uppermost in her mind, until she gets used to the new ones and sees their importance to her own success. Every employee, in the high-tech industry or elsewhere, has the obligation (in addition to any formal duties) to learn to manage his manager. This obligation is to himself, and it is a sine qua non of advancement in the corporate world. And rule number one in managing a manager is "no [unpleasant] surprises!" Managers *hate* hearing bad news, and if your manager learns from a third party and not from you yourself that you have become a member of such-and-such a working group, that could make you look like a loose cannon and make your manager look uninformed.

In general, it is not advisable to ask your manager's permission to start broadening your job, simply because it projects the image that you yourself are not certain whether you really want to do it, and that you're seeking encouragment. Also, asking permission turns you from a professional into a supplicant, never a good role for any employee in any industry. A young woman who works in a Silicon Valley hardware company said:

> An individual should not depend on the company or their manager to grow their job. That's the responsibility of the employee. So for me it may be going to school, which I'm doing. I'm getting my master's degree, and the company is paying for it because it's in a related field. For me it may also be making a list of professional books I want to complete. Or reading professional journals or attending professional organizations.

> Now certainly your manager can be aware of it and assist you where needed, giving the names of people in other departments if you're interested in moving over to another department, but you need to take the responsibility upon yourself versus depending on the company or your manager to help you move up.

This woman is actually engaged in expanding her knowledge base (adding new skills) in preparation for expanding her job.

Another woman who is an engineer decided how she realized she needed to start growing her job after she had been successfully working for several years. Her thoughts are pertinent to anyone working in the high-tech industry.

> You really always have to be looking at yourself and thinking, OK, what can I add to my arsenal that will make me more valuable to this company? This is something you should be doing all along. I know in the past I've ridden on the coattails of [a specific technology]. I became an expert in it and did nothing with it for a couple of years, and I finally had to wake up [when there were rumors of layoffs]. Sometimes these shakeups are good. I woke up and said, Wow, I need to teach myself some new skills because this is not going to carry me forward. [You need to] really look at your skill set and figure how to add to it, and look to the future of what's emerging.

> Fortunately there is all kinds of excellent literature around, so that's one way to upgrade. At a company like this one there is also a wealth of expertise of people, so if you can network or meet some of the people that are involved [with a new direction], that's probably most important. If you can get someone who's possibly already involved in the new area to sit down with you for a bit and give you some clues on how you might educate yourself, that's a start.

What you really do when you start growing your job is to begin developing career self-reliance. This is the single most valuble skill you can have in the high-tech industry. Again and again you will encounter this emphasis on self-reliance in the high-tech industry, and it correlates closely with the industry's growing reliance on the motivated and skilled individual contributor (who usually participates as a member of a team) rather than the middle manager. A technical editor says:

> [My direct reports] have a lot of autonomy. We have a career path for writers, and not surprisingly one thing that marks it is ability to work independently. And junior writers need a lot of supervision, and they really do need it. There are business implications, technical implications, just plain old writing practices, and so on. But as one gains experience, one can work much more independently. I have quite senior writers

working for me now, and I certainly want to review all their
plans and counsel them and help them make plans, but I almost never read the final product.

And this from one of her writers:

> The kinds of stuff I do are incredibly high profile, and I'm the
> only one that does them.

Here are some examples of growing one's job, to give you an idea
of what actually happens. Tony worked in the customer marketing department of a software company. His job was to assist the sales force in
Asia to license software to large OEMs by negotiating complex licensing
agreements; for this purpose he traveled to Asia five or six times a year.
He would explain the provisions of the agreement to the customers,
calling back to the United States for legal advice (he was not a lawyer)
where necessary. Tony wanted eventually to get into sales; the problem
was that he was doing a great job where he was, and the Asia sales force
particularly wanted him to stay in his present job. He told me:

> I was frustrated at first. Then I saw that we were getting these
> requests from Eastern Europe and Russia; all kinds of people
> wanted to visit us to learn about our products. No one at
> headquarters was interested, because they thought there was
> no money in those places. We had one sales guy covering all
> the ex-Communist countries on a part-time basis. So I de-
> cided to invite some of these groups to visit us, and I'd set up
> the agendas for the meetings and host them.

Tony started to get known as the person to whom all such requests
should come. When the part-time salesperson started negotiating some
serious deals in that part of the world, it turned out that Tony knew
many of the customers, having met them on their visits to company
headquarters. He was able to negotiate a position in the sales organization based in the United States, but with responsibility for developing
business in Eastern Europe and Russia.

Jenny worked for a very large computer company as a project coordinator in the company's equivalent of a public library, the technical
documentation group. She said:

> I was enjoying my job, but they were reorganizing, going to
> a centralized structure. I wanted to be a project leader (the
> next step up), but with this change I knew that wasn't going

to happen. And I also wanted to get out of technical documentation and start dealing with the actual products. So I found a project coordinator position in networking communications. I would have liked to have a project leader position, but I didn't think I could make that jump because I didn't have any experience that [management] would think was relevant. So what I did was, I went into this interview and I talked to a gentleman and said, "What I really want to do is be a project leader. But I want to start as a coordinator because I want to learn this business."

And from Day One that expectation was set. I did it on purpose—I really didn't want to be a project coordinator. Because I told him from the beginning I wanted to grow my job, I ended up getting hired for the position. There were a lot of people who wanted [it]. They had over a hundred resumés from within the company for two positions. After about six months I was actually [doing project leader work]. At the end of the next six months . . . they promoted me to project leader.

And the marketing manager for a small company that makes and sells specialized instruments to the computer industry describes how he grew his job from product manager for a single product:

I grew the job. I had been in sales, but then we had a bad couple of years and my income was cut in half. So I suggested that I move into marketing, and I became a product marketing manager. I started out with just the main-line product. Then we came out with a whole new product line with a different market, different customer set. We went to the venture capitalists and they put in lots of money. We started going to all the trade shows, spending a lot of money in promotion. I got involved in writing the sales training materials, and then in the promotion of the product. So then I had two lines and I was doing it all. I ended up as the company's marketing manager.

There's one danger you may face as you seek to grow your job, and that is that you may end up doing a lot of work that benefits others— your colleagues, or your boss, for example—but that does not add much to your own personal inventory of useful skills. In the high-tech industry, almost everyone has too much to do, and people will seek ways to offload some of this onto whoever appears willing and eager for more work. If this contributes to your strategic direction and adds to your contacts and knowledge (and if you don't get swamped by it), fine—take it on. If not, refuse to do it.

Making Effective Presentations

When you grow your job, you start to get involved in those areas of your division or department that involve new problems and opportunities. Because they're new, there is no well-defined approach to them, and so you're really breaking new ground. Chances are you'll be asked to make periodic reports on how you're doing. But if you're not, if it seems as if neither your boss nor your colleagues are very interested, be sure to arrange to inform them anyway. To do this, you call a meeting, assemble everyone whose work is or might be affected by what you're working on, and make a presentation to them. Use your judgment, but if it seems reasonable, have your manager attend as well, so that he or she can bask in the reflected glory of your accomplishments. (Always give your manager a private briefing beforehand so that there are no surprises!)

The effective presentation is the single best tool for achieving recognition and positioning yourself for advancement in the high-tech industry. It shows that you can tackle new areas of responsibility on your own and that you can pull in resources as needed from elsewhere in the company to achieve a solution. It is subtle, because you're not directly seeking any reward; you are reporting on your project. You may invite open discussion on which of two or three alternative paths is best for future work on the problem; you may request money or people to help you finish the job. Whatever the primary purpose of the presentation, there is always a secondary purpose: to present *you!*

Many presentations in the high-tech industry are uninteresting, overlong, choked with data, and badly delivered. So many are like this that a certain resigned tolerance has grown up. People filing into a conference room *expect* a presentation to be mediocre, and often they are not disappointed. This is too bad, because whether or not a bad presentation achieves its primary purpose, it usually fails in its secondary one: that of showing that you are a smart, confident, poised character who knows the subject matter cold and who is probably destined for higher things some day.

Most presentations in the high-tech industry are put together at the last minute; it's usual to see a nervous admin running from his system to the printer, hastily revising overhead transparencies and running off twenty, or thirty, or fifty hardcopies of the whole thing, to be passed

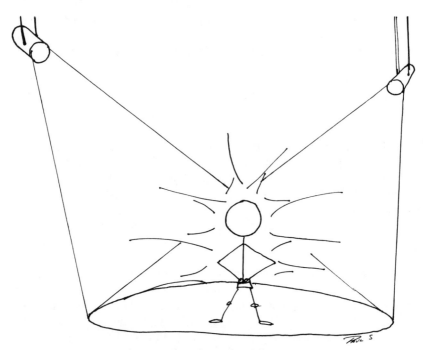

Your presentations should star *you!*

out to all those attending the meeting. In fact, it is bemusing to contemplate the vast quantities of paper that are used up in a high-tech presentation, given that technology is supposed to liberate us from paper flow. One of the most engaging sights to the detached observer of important presentations in the industry is that of the presenter standing to the side of a screen, using a pointer to take the audience through a crowded slide, while the audience has its collective head down and is apparently attentively reading the same slide in the handout. As the slide on the screen changes, there is the sound of twenty or so individual pages being turned in as many handouts. Another attraction of the mediocre presentation is to hear the presenter reading, word for word, and line for line, the contents of each slide, expanding on a given topic as he or she thinks the situation may demand. In larger presentations in the high-tech industry it's not unheard of for the sales force to be found at the rear of the hall assiduously working on expense reports.*

It is not hard to give a good presentation once you are properly

---

*There's no good place in the text to insert this important point, so I'll say it here: If you are in a high-tech job where you spend the company's money and submit expense reports, always do this accurately and *on time!* Having a reputation for this will distinguish you favorably in your boss's mind.

prepared. Many companies offer courses in presentation skills, and it is very important to sign up for one if you have the chance. If you don't have such an opportunity in your company, perhaps you can find one at a continuing education center somewhere nearby. If you can't, here are the Seven Commandments for making outstanding presentations.

Seven Commandments

1. *Organize your subject.* You have to *think* before you start making up your slides. You want this thing to have a beginning, a middle, and an end. It should look something like this:

   A. What I'm Going to Tell you:
      - First point
      - Second point
      - Third point
   B. Now I'm Telling You:
      - First point (expanded)
        —Subsidiary point one
        —Subsidiary point two
        —(Perhaps) subsidiary point three
      - Second point (expanded)
        —Subsidiary point one, etc.
      - Third point (expanded)
        —Subsidiary point one, etc.
   C. The Result of What I've Told You:
      - (E.g.) Where we stand today
      - The two (or three, etc.) alternatives
      - Resources needed to continue progress
      - Remaining milestones

So you should do an outline, and you want to stick to three major points in your presentation. There's an old rule in consulting: Always give 'em three. Why not two, or four? Three engages the interest more; two points invite argument, and four invite confusion.

When you go into an important presentation, take a one-page outline with you. It'll be a lifesaver if you lose your way.

2. *Less is more.* Everyone in the high-tech industry seems to honor this rule in the breach rather than the observance. Most high-tech presentations are too long and have too much data, too many slides and handouts, and too much on each slide. They don't seem ever to focus in on the point of the whole exercise. Their value is mostly soporific.

Keep slides clean! Use bullets, and keep your text to five or six lines per slide and a few words per bullet. It's great discipline to try to do this; it gets you really understanding your subject matter, and it keeps you from reading the whole presentation from the screen.

If you have half an hour for a presentation, do it in twenty minutes and then invite discussion. Your audience will be surprised and delighted, and then will get really involved with the topic.

3. *Maintain control.* If your audience's attention wanders, of if two people in the back of the room start a private conversation, stop talking and stand motionless. After about five seconds you will have everyone's full attention.

If you've planned ten to twenty minutes for discussion, say so at the beginning of the presentation and then stick to it. Obviously if your boss's boss is listening and wants to ask a question, you'll have to answer it, but avoid getting drawn into side discussions until the end.

4. *Pace yourself.* Many high-tech presentations are planned for half an hour, but the presenter arrives with fifty overheads. The audience is then subjected to an in situ attempt to edit the presentation, complete with mumblings such as, "Naw, I don't think that'll be useful." If you know you've got thirty minutes, do your presentation at home the night before, in front of a mirror, or your spouse, or the cat; but get it to thirty minutes! Twenty is better, as mentioned above.

5. *Be calm and look at your audience.* One presenter at a high-tech conference had the peculiar habit of waltzing every time he began speaking. He would slide his left foot forward, then lean to the right and move his right foot to the right. Next he would bring his left foot over to the right, and then slide the right foot back. There were about 200 people in the room; those toward the rear could only see the effects this movement had on his head and shoulders, while those in the front could admire the full effect. No one paid much attention to what he was saying.

The only way to cure a case like this is through practicing relaxing while talking, and using a video camera or friends for feedback. It's the hardest thing in the world to simply stand still on a stage or podium, with your arms at your sides, and talk to people.

It's important to maintain eye contact with *individual* members of the audience as you make your presentation. Change individuals from time to time, of course. You can be sure that anyone you are watching will be paying strict attention to what you are saying, but the real purpose of this gimmick is to keep a bond between you and the entire audience.

6. *When things go wrong, don't panic.* There's a saying in the world of actors, the audience never knows unless you tell them. That means that when you screw up or lose your way, it's not a big deal for your listeners

unless you clue them that it's a big deal. When President Clinton gave a very important address of his presidency, introducing his proposed health care plan to Congress and to the nation in September 1993, no one realized that he was ad-libbing for the first five minutes. Some hapless aide had put the wrong speech on the teleprompter.

Similarly, an actor playing the character of Charles was in the middle of the second act of a stage production of Noel Coward's *Blithe Spirit* when he realized that he had unwittingly slipped ahead and was giving lines from the third act. (There is a remarkable similarity between many of the lines in the two acts.) He managed to slide back into the second act, to the vast relief of the rest of the cast. But the interesting thing is that almost no one in the audience noticed that anything was wrong.

When things go wrong in a presentation (and normally that means you've lost your train of thought), just stop, take a breath, take a "drink of your notes," and start in again.

7. *Announce the end of the presentation.* You can do this by using phrases such as "finally" or "to summarize." And if your boss's boss is there, always thank the audience for coming.

Using Mentors

A mentor is a person who helps you be at ease with your environment, your colleagues, and your work by listening sympathetically and by giving you advice from time to time. Almost every person interviewed for this book mentioned the importance of having a mentor. Some high-tech companies even have formal mentoring programs, something I am unaware of in any other branch of industry. Most people mentioned having mentors inside their company, but some turned to people in companies they had formerly worked for. What they seek is the perspective of someone who has wrestled with the same types of problems they are confronting, and with whom a deep bond of trust has been established.

Why mentoring should be so important in the high-tech world as to be institutionalized is a subject for conjecture. I believe that like so much else that differentiates the industry from others, it is related to the fast pace and erratic path that technology takes, and the fact that entire large organizations are trying to react in real time to the "paradigm shifts." Mentors provide support, encouragement, and understanding without having anything to gain other than the good feeling that comes from helping you over the rough spots.

A woman who has been in the same company since she started working six years ago had this to say about mentors:

There are sort of the official mentors, called [the official name], and there are unofficial mentors, or people who take you under their wing. I have to say the official mentors do things like show you where to get forms and all that sort of thing. But that's not necessarily what's important. The important thing is the individuals who have sort of figured out how to work in [company], which is being aggressive and finding out how to get things done and who knows people across the company. That's the other thing I've found out over the six years. . . . I started in this group and we were sort of in a cocoon, didn't really know a lot of people on the outside. All these people I used to work with are now all over the company, and it's made a tremendous difference—figuring out how to get things done when you can just call up somebody you used to work with and ask them. I think there is probably a lot of mentoring that goes on unofficially.

Making Lateral Transfers

A lateral transfer refers to your making a move to another job within the company when the new job is at the same level as the old one—in other words, where no promotion is involved. Traditionally, corporate employees started their careers with the expectation that hard work and outstanding performance would result in a move up the corporate ladder. Lateral moves within the company (or to another company) were perceived as fruitless, a waste of energy, even an admission of failure.

That perception is changing. You know that the corporate structure in America has traditionally been a pyramid, with hordes of low-level workers supporting middle management, which in turn supports higher management. At the very top are the officers of the company. But in the high-tech world that is all changing very rapidly. Elsewhere I've referred to the flattening of the high-tech company and the tremendous emphasis that is being placed on the individual contributor. Since the pyramid has been flattened, the corporate ladder that was supposed to help you scale the slopes has been turned on its side. Now what is important to the company is that you do a great job where you are, and you've already seen that "doing a great job" really means growing your job. But what is important to *you* is also moving from your job to somewhere else in the high-tech company, thus broadening your skills and your network, and recharging your batteries with brand new challenges.

Many high-tech industry people today feel frustrated that they have not been promoted to the next rung. This is really a waste of energy.

These days, often the "next rung" either doesn't exist or may not in the near future. A human resources manager told me:

> Middle management is an area that won't survive. As organizations continue to downsize and continue to take costs out of the system, middle management will be the primary target, and it's happened already.

What you really should be concerned with is how much money you are making and how much your contribution is valued by your manager and your team, not what your job title is. It's true that higher-level managers, starting at the level called "director" in the high-tech industry, have bonus plans that lower-level individuals do not. But it's also true that directors and higher-level managers do not ipso facto have greater job security; they can and do get downgraded and even fired. They also have to attend regular meetings that can seem interminable; they may have to sit through the whole day, where as you as an individual contributor can come in, make a twenty-minute presentation on some business problem, and leave everybody impressed and refreshed by your command of the issue. And it is not pleasant to be one of a few hundred directors in a large corporation and learn from a memo out of the president's office that come next January there will be 50 percent fewer directors than there are today!

Lateral transfers are usually very rewarding in terms of renewed work satisfaction. The following comments came from a woman who was reviewing her career at her former employer, a hardware company; she had just accepted a job in a smaller software company.

> I happen to need challenges in large doses on a regular basis, and I need variety and change. So I learn things and I get bored very quickly.

She had four jobs in about seven years, and was now seeking an environment that would offer her even more varied opportunities.

I do not mean to imply that one comes into the high-tech company and has to remain at the same job level forever. Changing jobs within a company does occasionally offer the opportunity for a promotion, and even within your existing work group, if you've grown your job and let your manager know about it, your job can be "releveled," resulting in a promotion for you. When this happens, it's great for you, because there is no competition for the higher-level job—it's yours already. When someone in a job leaves the company, however, and you want to go after that position, which is now vacant, you're likely to discover that there is intense competition from several other people. Even if it's the same level for you, it may represent a promotion for them. You'll have to sell yourself to the hiring manager just as you would if you were coming from the outside, except that you now are an insider with a track record, and you have people who will go to bat for you.

If you really want to try for the managerial ranks, it may be that your best opportunity will be in a different high-tech company. You've spent some years acquiring a broad range of experience, and you may think you have much to contribute in determining your company's strategic direction and find that no one who counts will listen to you. The Bible says that a prophet is not without honor, save in his own country. That being the case, you may wish to change countries. A man who had been with the same computer company for seven years, and whose last position was manager of relations with ISVs, reflected on this:

> I've accepted that it's nice to be at a company for a long time, but in the high-tech industry things change quickly, and staying at any company for more than five years can be detrimental to one's career. Therefore I'm not going to commit myself [to his new employer] the same way I did here. I don't mind changing companies. If I stay with the next company for three years, I'll be happy.

Continuing Your Education

In Chapter 5, which discusses culture, you've already seen how the high-tech industry values training and retraining. You'll probably have the right to take one or two courses per quarter within the company or outside the company if there are only limited training opportunities within the company. You should be sure to take advantage of these. You can pick up some in-depth technology; you can also learn lots about effective management, such as how to hire and fire, how to manage in ways that respect gender and ethnic diversity, how to negotiate, and so forth. It's not necessary to add these to your resumé, but they will make you a more mature and able businessperson.

Many high-tech employees are "too busy" to take advantage of training and educational opportunities. This is really too bad, because it demonstrates warped priorities. You can always stay late or work weekends to complete a project; but the more you keep putting off that course, the more your career goes along without the advantages it can bring. So fix a date, keep it on your calendar, and just do it!

Summarizing all the wisdom set forth above, to thrive in high-tech, you've got to do five things:

1. Grow your job.
2. Get visibility through presentations.
3. Develop and use mentors.
4. Make lateral moves.
5. Continue your education.

These five actions will ensure not only that you'll thrive in the high-tech environment, but also that you'll never be bored.

Long-Term Survival

Why raise the topic of survival at all? If you are thriving in your job, is there any reason to doubt that you can survive on the job as long as you wish? Unfortunately, there is. When you start your employment, you may hear a lot about being a valued member of the team, and about how XYZ Corporation is "employee-driven." But industrywide, all this is changing. While your particular employer may have retained the nurturance culture, this can give you a false sense of security. The greatest manifestation of the nurturance culture has been the unspoken commitment by management and employee to lifetime employment. This was strongest in the older high-tech companies such as DEC and IBM, and it was almost as strong as that of the large Japanese companies.

Events in the last few years have ended this dream, and led to anguished reappraisal of the concept of nurturance by both management and employees. Poor management decisions, a recession, the evolution of technology, competitive pressures, and above all a failure to adapt to rapidly changing market demands have wrought economic havoc with many older high-tech firms. An IBM executive observed recently, "When you came into IBM, it was a company you worked for until you retired. Today you work for it until you are declared surplus." But there is nostalgia for the old days, and pride in the IBM way, as the executive recounts how IBM tries to help the thousands of employees recently laid off.

> The process is, well, it's more severe than it was last year, but the process is, 'Gee, Tom, I'm sorry I don't have a job for you right now. Would you like to take this [retirement package], or would you like us to look for another job for you? Last year the program was, "We'll come to you with a job offer." This

year it's, "I'm not sure I can find you a job offer, but I'm damned well going to work at it. We may find you a lousy job, because that's all we've got right now. You may decide to resign anyway." Well, yes, to you and your wife you were laid off. But we didn't just give you a slip and say, "See you later!"

In other words, we will go through a ritual, at the end of which you will be unemployed, but that ritual demonstrates that we care for you and that the IBM ethos still survives. Unfortunately, even that ritual may not be far from oblivion.

Younger, healthier high-tech companies also want to believe that the company nurturance of employees hasn't entirely vanished in the era of "downsizing." The vice-president for human resources of such a company recently said:

> What was possible in the 1980s in terms of protection of jobs and so forth is, in the competitive environment we're in today, not possible any more. So therefore jobs are at risk, and therefore your job [as a member of HR] is to ensure that the interests of the majority of the enterprise are looked after. If that necessitates a reduction in force, that is achieved in a fair manner, and the company culture is represented in the way people are treated.

What we are observing here is the disappearance of the nurturance culture under the pressures affecting all high-tech enterprises. Once the company is seen to be backing off from its once apparently unshakable devotion to its employees' continued employment and welfare, the employees naturally feel their psychological bonds to the company weakening. And when, as in the case of IBM and DEC, thousands or tens of thousands of loyal employees are fired, when entire departments are closed down, many who are left on the job experience the same shock and trauma as those who survive an airplane crash or other major disaster—fear, guilt, and thankfulness all at once. One would naturally assume that loyalty among these employees would go out the window, and that they would instantly begin preparing their own effective emergency survival or bailout plans. But they do not. Most employees who grew up in the nurturance culture find it impossible to change their attitude and to take effective preventive action. They enter a state of denial, which is highly dangerous. Their survival plans all assume that help will be forthcoming from within their company. This is never the case. When a company starts a downsizing campaign, it is in response to its own survival imperative. The board fires the old management and brings in a new CEO and others who have no intention of continuing the nurturance culture so far as job security is concerned.

Employees who fail to analyze their situations dispassionately and to act accordingly only postpone the inevitable. I had a conversation with a man who had come to California from England to be the vice-president for human resources of a growing software company. This man had sold his home and most of his possessions rather than storing them, because his plan was to stay five years in the new job. When his children were ready for higher education, he planned to return to England, cashing in his stock options and selling his house, which was appreciating at about 30 percent per year.

After about a year, his U.S. employer began experiencing financial problems and had to reduce the workforce. The vice-president of human resources worked to do this in a sensitive way, trying to soften the shock to those being laid off. Then the financial news got worse, and the vice-president again worked long hours trying to help those laid off to get good references and leads to new jobs. In the third wave of layoffs, the vice-president found himself on the street. He told me:

> I guess I knew how bad things were. I was in most of those meetings [where the financial situation was discussed]. But I buried myself in trying to help others. It was inconceivable that it could happen to me, because I just had too much to lose.

This admirable man returned to England with his family, where he remained unemployed for several months. He finally got a job but remained depressed for a long time.

Maintaining Your Successful Career

What you must do is periodically review where you are in terms of your skills and present job activities, and match these with your analysis of where the company is going and what you'll need to make the journey with it. When you do this analysis, you should consult with your manager and with others at his or her level. Get their ideas about what is happening in the industry and what you can do to acquire new skills to enable you to survive and grow. What you learn may not help you very much; they may be as confused as you are about these issues. But you will have demonstrated that you are aware that changes are taking place. You'll get a reputation for being alert and flexible, two key attributes for survival, and this reputation alone will serve you well.

You'll also want to make full use of relevant training opportunities as they become available. Get to know someone in the training department; new skills courses are usually run through a free beta-testing phase, and you can get in on them without your department's being charged. Then you can report on them to your manager and your group, again adding to your reputation.

If you feel that your company is on the wrong track, that it has missed too many opportunities, that it has hired too many of the wrong sorts of people for higher management positions, that it has changed in fundamental ways that make you uncomfortable, or that its future looks doubtful, start heading for Plan B. Contact your network of individuals in other companies; let it be known you'd be interested in learning of opportunities. Talk to a headhunter or two, and take an occasional look at the classified section of the paper. It will not take you long to find good alternative employment, because you are currently employed, and to those in other companies who interview you, you are therefore perceived as more valuable than people who are on unemployment benefits or who are temporarily working as "consultants."

Everything is a tradeoff—moving to another company means that you'll have to start building credibility all over again. But you'll come in at a higher level and a better salary (don't make a move if these aren't part of the deal).

Be a team player in your present job by all means, but never forget that first and foremost you have to be a rugged individualist. "Looking out for Number One" is a very appropriate attitude these days in the high-tech industry.

7
Startups

Why talk about startups in a book about high-tech careers? Because startups are fascinating, exciting, sexy, and where many employees in the high-tech industry start dreaming of being after a few years on the job. Because those who get in on the ground floor have the chance to take risks and maybe become rich. Because startups have no bureaucracy, little structure, and no processes that have to be followed. Because those working in startups are writing the book as they go; if they do things right, there's no one higher up the ladder who is going to grab any of the credit, because there *is* no ladder. If they do things wrong, the company is going to fail, as many do.

American high-tech business lore is full of stories about startups: companies that started in someone's garage or apartment, that "went public," and that grew to dominate whole segments of the high-tech industry, making their founders wildly rich in the process. Apple is one of the best known of the successful startups. Sun Microsystems is another. The most interesting thing about the startup story is that it is continuing today. All one has to do is consult a high-tech directory such as *Rich's High Tech Business Guide* to see how many small companies have been founded in the last five years or so in various regions of the United States. And as you'll see in a while, there is often a role for nontechnical people in the startup. If you are into excitement, risk, long hours, variety, and unpredictability in your work, if the startup looks viable, and if you are a bit of a gambler to boot, then you should go for it! It's possible that you'll make a very large amount of money. You'll certainly gain a lot of varied experience and have a lot of fun.

When does a company stop being a startup? Opinions differ on this; some people think it's when the company first ships a product, and others require that the company be profitable. From the point of view of the employees, it is probably as much a question of psychology as anything else. The startup feeling can last for a few years, well after the

Start-ups are risky . . . and exciting!

company becomes profitable, provided it succeeds in retaining most of
its original employees.

Getting a Startup Started

Startups get started when someone has an idea and isn't content just to
leave it at that. The idea could involve any aspect of the high-tech industry, though probably the majority of startups today are involved with
software. Though the folklore startup hero is by tradition a college drop-
out, most people who launch small high-tech companies have spent
some years working for large high-tech companies. They take their idea
and share it with two or three others; they massage and shape it, get an
idea of the market once it is commercialized, and quit their jobs to be-

come entrepreneurs. Of course, they have to have access to capital; sometimes initial capital comes from savings, relatives, and friends. Eventually, though, major funding is needed, and the founders usually must attempt to get this from commercial sources. In the 1980s risk capital could actually be obtained from banks; today that is no longer possible, as banks demand security, which the fledgling company does not have. The startup therefore attempts to get funding from venture capital (VC) firms. In order to do so, the founders draw up a business plan that shows how the company plans to develop, manufacture, and sell its products. The plan includes the history of the founders of the startup, since the venture capital firm will depend on their technical knowhow and business acumen for the success of the investment.

What are the chances of a startup's getting venture capital funding? The head of a VC firm said recently:

> In one year at the end of the 1980s we looked at about 700 proposals. We decided to fund four of them. Two of these have gone sour already.

But he went on to add that he was very satisfied with the two remaining; they were performing well, which could translate eventually into huge profits for the VC firm.

The wise startup entrepreneur will have made an effort to get some impressive names on the board of directors; these people can provide introductions into the VC community, as well as giving credibility to the startup.

When a venture capital firm decides to invest in a startup, it usually has a seat on the board, and often more than one. This enables the VC firm to keep its finger on the pulse of the business as it develops. In high-tech startups, after four or five years there is usually a push from the board for liquidity, that is, to take the company public. At this point the investment banks get involved. Such institutions have specialized sales forces that are looking for companies that might be ready to go public. A representative of such a bank told me:

> We are constantly out there looking at companies, and we make the initial decision whether this is interesting enough to bring in an analyst. We get involved at the top of the company. They usually have a corporate presentation they do for us, and we ask them a lot of questions. If it's interesting, I'll come back with my analyst in a week or so. Then we ask them for their financials. If we don't think a company is doing well, we won't take it public.

The investment bank looks at everything—the competition, how big the markets are, the company's strategy and how well it appears to be executing it, what technological advantages it has, and what is proprietary. "Proprietary" in this context means a significant market advantage that other people haven't been able to copy. Neither VC firms nor investment banks are very interested in PC startups these days, because the PC is becoming a "commodity," a product where it is difficult to show any proprietary advantage, and indeed where being proprietary is a disadvantage (see Chapter 4, "Computers in Ten Minutes"). It is very possible that in some investment banks, the consumer products division rather than the high-tech division may be interested in looking at PC companies.

When the high-tech startup is taken public, the stock tends to be priced at between $10 and $20 per share; a typical valuation of the company itself might be upwards of $75 million. That would be the market value of the equity at the beginning of the transaction.

Working in a High-Tech Startup

Even most people working in the high-tech industry believe that a startup can afford to take on only very technical people. The company is under extreme pressure to bring out a successful product, and it is generally believed that there's simply no place for a nontechnical person. But although this may be true at the very beginning, this situation doesn't last very long. Many startups have taken on nontechnical people when the total staff of the company was thirty people or less.

What do such people do? One woman in her thirties who is in the financial department of a growing software company of some 300 people in the Boston area told me:

> When I started here, I did everything. I did accounts payable and receivable, payroll, shipping, receiving, bought the lunches. They already had a janitor, so I didn't clean the bathrooms. I was the eighth person hired. Everybody else was a programmer or a marketing guy, and I did everything else.

A marketing person in a hardware company said:

> We got started in an apartment. When I came in, I did filing, clerical stuff. There were about twelve people here then.

The principal reason most persons are attracted to startups is that their size means an informal and varied work life. An HR administrator in a small software company put it this way:

When I was here four years ago, we had trouble getting people to do expense reports because it smacked of bureaucracy.
The people that were here didn't like large companies, didn't
like red tape. The small-company atmosphere really attracted
them. The fact that to do their job they probably had to do
pieces of four other jobs attracted them.

And from another startup employee:

Part of the reason I like a small company is if you want to get
something done, you go to the person who you think can do
it and you talk to them. You don't have to go through channels and around barn doors and upstairs and downstairs.

So being in a startup involves doing a lot of different things in an
informal and fast-moving environment. And there's the added piquancy
of risk—because needless to say, not all startups survive.

Startup Mortality

Many startups do not make it past infancy, and for those that do there
lurks a host of childhood diseases for which no vaccine seems effective.
People in high tech who think about startups—and that means almost
everyone—spend the occasional lunch hour discussing why such and
such a firm went under, or what the prospects are for good old Sam,
who left two months ago to launch Softsmash, Inc. In retrospect everyone can explain quite cogently why a healthy teenage company survived
the perils of youth, but no one can predict with any confidence whether
any given startup will succeed, no matter how brilliant and hardworking
the founders, how brilliant the idea, how well funded the effort, and
how eager the market. There are simply too many variables, so that it is
usually concluded that luck has to be with you as well.

What is the mortality rate of high-tech startups? No one knows this
for certain, either, but probably no more than five out of a hundred will
survive more than three years. Perhaps two of these will survive past
the age of six. In the normal, non-high-tech world, being associated with
a company that goes belly-up sometimes carries a sort of stigma; the
company failed, so those who started it and who were employed by it
must somehow also be failures. No such stigma is attached to the failure
of a high-tech startup, simply because everyone knows, from the high-
tech media to the VC firms, from the headhunters to the bartenders at
high-tech watering holes, that a high-tech startup is a risky business.

People in the high-tech industry admire those who have an idea and are willing to back it all the way, even if that means all the way to bankruptcy court. As a startup employee said:

> Everybody has their strong suit. You could do well starting a company, have the vision to start a company based on a product, and not have the skill set to grow it. And that doesn't mean you're a bad person. There are many more people who don't have the vision to start a company.

Getting a Job in a Startup

Whether a startup survives through infancy does depend in part on how well it manages its initial growth. Often this calls for a skill set that the founders may not have. Founders usually concentrate on product development, whereas success and growth ultimately involve every activity mentioned in Chapter 2, "The Jobs." Of course, a tiny company cannot afford all the people needed to do all these tasks, but neither can it afford to ignore them for very long. Startups' founders often have a very clear idea of the market for their first product, but this is usually only sufficient to get the startup past the first year or so of production. That is often the entry point for a nontechnical employee.

You can discover many startup opportunities if you are already employed in a high-tech company. It's easy if you have friends in engineering disciplines. They'll know that such and such a person who just left has started a company or joined up with so and so who started a firm last year. Word gets about. Startups need all kinds of help, from menial tasks to marketing, bookkeeping, and sales. The route in is almost always through a friend who gets involved and then brings you in. If the startup has only a handful of employees, you'll have to meet them all and pass muster with everyone. If it's been around for a year or two and has, say, fifty employees, you won't have to be voted in by everyone.

There are two ways to get involved with a startup. The first is at the very beginning. If you have no obligations to others (spouse, children, other dependents) and don't owe too much on your credit cards, you can try to be employee number ten at the startup. Salary? Not much, but maybe enough barely to survive. Most of the compensation at this stage may be in stock options—convertible into stock after the company goes public. On the other hand, if the company is well funded by venture capital, perhaps you can get something more like a decent salary.

The other way to get into a startup is a bit later, when there appears to be a good chance that the company will survive. Stock options may not be as plentiful at this stage, but there should still be plenty. In a typical case, in the early 1990s a young man joined a software company as an hourly employee doing rather routine tasks. His total compensation the first year was about $20,000, not including some overtime, but he received a vested interest in 1,500 shares in the company. For each of the next three years, provided he remains on the job, he will receive another 1,500 shares. After one year he received a raise of only 3 percent, but was granted an additional 1,000 shares of stock. Assuming that the company survives and he stays with it and that the same level of largesse is maintained, he could end up with 10,000 shares at the end of four years. He and his colleagues are hoping that the company will go public, that the value of the stock will soar, and that they can cash out at some point with a nice gain.

Beyond Money

Working in a startup gives you fantastic exposure to many aspects of the high-tech business world. If it gets too rough, you can always come in from the cold into a large company—people do this all the time. You'll have your network in place, and you'll have experience. A middle-aged woman who got into high-tech startups after having spent some years as a housewife had this to say to those who get involved with startups:

> Don't give up. This is my third startup. The first two didn't make it. The first one reached 130 people and died. The second wasn't ever going to be that big . . . we reached about twenty-two people, and then it was clear we weren't going to make it. That place is where I knew the president of this company from. So when he got involved in this one and they needed a support person, he called me.
>
> The mortality rate can be pretty high, but just because one doesn't work, don't let it sour you on trying another if that's the type of culture and environment you're comfortable in. Worst case, even if the company doesn't make it, you've had a job. Hopefully they've been solvent enough so they can make payroll, but you've been making contacts all the time, and you're growing your skills unbelievably.

This person mentioned the "culture and environment" of the startup. After working for a few years in the high-tech industry, some employees get restless: The company has grown "too large" and they don't feel comfortable any more. This is a standard complaint heard in hardware and software companies from those who've been there since the early days. Often such people look for (and find) employment at a startup, where they feel less trammeled by rules and regulations. You know yourself better than anyone else does; if you, too, start getting itchy feet, you should seriously consider getting into the world of startups. In the words of a friend who puts in long hours trying to pull his startup through to success:

> I'm too tired to be terrified. And I've never had so much fun in my life!

8
Going International

General Considerations

Most high-tech companies do some part of their business with customers outside the United States. It would be surprising if this were not the case, since the United States is clearly the world leader in high-tech innovation and commercialization. Perhaps the only companies that don't engage in international business are very small, very young companies that simply don't have the knowhow to get into overseas markets and don't yet have the staff to get started. If you are interested in getting into international business, you're probably wondering what opportunities the high-tech industry has for you.

Basically there are three types of international work in the high-tech industry. In the first, one is based in the United States, but the job requires frequent traveling overseas. At the individual contributor level this is usually a sales or channels management job. In the second type of international work, you are again resident in this country, but with infrequent travel abroad. There are many such positions, including marketing, legal, finance, sales support, contract negotiations, and account management positions in a high-tech company's international division (if you have such a position in a corporate headquarters division, your chances of international travel are less). This chapter does not address this sort of position, because these days *any* of the jobs listed in Chapter 2 could involve some international travel.

The third type of international job is one that involves an overseas posting, and it's that type that this chapter is mostly concerned with. These jobs are also found in a variety of functional areas—more if the company is in a phase of "moving functions out to the field," less if the company is retrenching and pulling functions back to headquarters. If getting into international work is your prime objective in getting into high-tech, you ought to find out which stage your particular target company is in, expansion or contraction. Be assured, though, that these things go in cycles, and that even in a company that is pulling back there will be opportunity for overseas work at some point.

Overseas Assignments

What is the position in general of the high-tech industry today, with respect to sending Americans overseas? Here is the response of a long-time international HR manager:

> [In the past] I felt that it was essential that our American employees [get overseas].
>
> But that was a few years ago. Now we're in more competitive times and everyone is questioning all areas of cost, what the return on investment is in these expatriate assignments. It's very difficult to quantify the return. So now people are questioning every overseas assignment and suggesting it's not a good thing to do.

Indeed, it's now very hard to get a traditional overseas assignment in the high-tech industry, for reasons of cost. It costs a company between $300,000 and $500,000 a year to send an "expat" overseas, depending on the country. If these figures leave you incredulous, consider what a first-class apartment costs in Hong Kong (end-1993). The rent is $10,000 a month. That's U.S., not Hong Kong, dollars. It may be necessary to pay one to two years' rent in advance, and of course that does not include any furnishings. Furnishings have to be either purchased locally or shipped from the United States. If they are shipped from the United States, the cost will be immense for the usual allowance of 6,000 pounds, which is not enough to furnish a whole house. Of course this does not include major appliances, which are usually purchased locally (if available) because of voltage differences. Other expat costs can include private schools for children (a necessity in some places, including Hong Kong); managing the rental of the U.S. home; loss on selling cars (or storage of cars); tax advisers' fees; cost-of-living adjustments; hardship post adjustments; hotel, transportation, and restaurant costs while searching for a suitable overseas dwelling (and while waiting for furnishings to arrive); cost of an automobile in the local country (often two to three times the cost of an equivalent vehicle in the United States); air fares to and from the assignment as well as home leaves or vacations; air fares of college-age children to and from the overseas post; medical evacuation insurance; storage of household goods while on assignment; and so forth.

Given these costs, it is understandable that companies have cut way back on the number of expatriate assignments. Right now the financial bean counters have the upper hand. But if you want to go overseas with the high-tech industry, it is absolutely possible to work this. You'll read how later on in this chapter. The good news is that the reasons why it makes sense to send American employees overseas still exist: to spread the corporate culture and, above all, to bring to international operations a familiarity with how things really get done back home, so that the system will work.

What High-Tech Firms Do Overseas

High-tech firms do three kinds of things at overseas locations. First, they have hardware manufacturing operations. In many countries it's possible to hire a line worker for a manufacturing plant for a daily wage that is less than an American worker makes in an hour. This is why so many traditional manufacturing jobs are leaving the United States—and other countries with expensive labor, such as Japan—for "offshore" locations. Though the public usually assumes that most of these jobs are in the low-skills category, this is not always so. Countries such as Korea and Singapore are home to sophisticated manufacturing operations calling for skilled workers. China and Taiwan are rapidly becoming known as locations where high-tech equipment can be easily produced to a world-class standard of quality. Many other countries, such as Mexico and Indonesia, are taking steps to invite high-tech firms to establish manufacturing operations.

High-tech companies also have established software development joint ventures with Indian companies. India is known throughout the high-tech world as a source of excellence in software development. In the United States a good software developer costs a company about $75,000 a year, including benefits. In India a developer of the same quality costs about $8,000 a year. A very large proportion of the software development industry will move offshore from the United States in India in coming years; this movement is already well under way, and has been facilitated by the Indian government's lowering of barriers to investment and repatriation of profits and capital by foreign firms.

The third type of activity that American high-tech firms carry out overseas is of more importance to nontechnical persons. It involves sales and marketing of products.

Sales

Sales representatives are usually, but not always, local nationals. Americans from the home office may be placed overseas in sales positions for any or all of the following reasons:

- They know the product and have experience in how to sell it, and for competitive reasons the company needs to move rapidly into the market.
- They have special knowledge of an important market segment, such as banking, and it will take time to train a local salesperson or locate one with equivalent knowledge.
- There is already a large local sales force, and one or more "role models" are needed to demonstrate how the company does business.
- The company wishes to give a sales rep exposure to international business before promoting him or her to a management position.
- The local sales force is young and lacks credibility in the marketplace; a representative from "headquarters" is needed to make joint sales calls to build credibility.
- The competition uses Americans to project how important it considers the market; the company has to match the competition.
- The market has hitherto been serviced from the United States, and the sales representative is now being posted overseas until the transition to a local sales force can be made.
- The overseas sales office is a regional office servicing many countries, and local nationals are not welcome in some of these countries.

Financial people look at international sales figures and how much it cost the company to attain them. Then they look at the breakdown of cost components and notice that the biggest elements are the cost of fancy overseas offices (rent, furnishing, renovation, utilities) and the cost of manpower. When they see that, for example, there are fifty local employees costing a total of $1 million and ten expatriate employees costing a total of $3 million, and they report this to top management, the word may go out to cut the expats down to two and reduce the office area by 25 percent. This is precisely the stage that many high-tech companies are in at present. The financial analysis, however, usually does not include any weighting of the relative contribution of the expats to total sales dollars. The effect of the cutbacks is not yet felt in the overall revenue figures.

Marketing

It makes good sense to locate marketing activities in the market they address, and this area offers nontechnical people an opportunity to work overseas. Some high-tech companies try to create advertising, public relations, and promotional programs in the United States, even when these are supposed to serve international markets. The idea seems to be that money can be saved by piggybacking on programs developed for the U.S. market. This idea rarely pans out, although unfortunately feedback mechanisms that might convey this message often either don't exist or are discounted by the company's headquarters marketing organization.

The way to get into international marketing overseas is to start out in the company's international headquarters in the United States and learn as much as possible about how the company is missing the boat in its overseas markets. You do this by becoming friendly with the salespeople who are servicing those markets, whether from the United States or in an international post. You also find out more by talking with customers who come on visits to the company. It's possible to build up a strong portfolio of arguments why your company should have a marketing arm located in a regional overseas office. How you actually make the sale to your top management is a matter we'll cover in a little while.

Other Functions

Many high-tech companies have regional offices overseas, and these regional offices may have expatriate positions in finance, legal, operations, and human resources. The regional office coordinates business in many countries where the high-tech company may have distributors and other resellers, or even a direct sales force. So it is possible to get a posting in such a position.

Exporting the Company's Culture

Up to 1990, when times were booming, it was not unheard of for individual contributors and managers to be sent overseas to bring some of the company's culture into the local office. A sales manager who spent two years on an overseas assignment tells why he was recruited by Tom, the head of the overseas operation:

> When Tom went to [the country], he wanted to bring a few
> people over that in his mind could really help infuse the spirit
> of the company and the excitement and all those intangible

things. I think he realized shortly after he got there that a lot of that was missing. There was none of our culture there; it was too far away. . . . It was all staffed by locals that had never had the opportunity to grow up through the exciting years at [the company]. So the idea was to bring in enough people so you could start things fermenting, like adding a little starter dough.

That's not terribly likely to become common again in the overseas offices of American companies until the industry enters a new period of explosive growth. It does happen frequently, however, within the European Community: An Irishman takes a position in Germany, a Frenchman in England. Distances are short, and costs of reassignment are low. And it happens in assignments between the United States, Mexico, and Canada.

Newcomers

It is very difficult to be a newcomer to the high-tech industry, even with international experience garnered elsewhere, and realistically expect to be in the running for an overseas assignment. Over the years I've been approached by U.S. Foreign Service officers and others with substantial experience, people who speak one or more foreign languages well, and even some who understand the industry and its international business issues as well as is possible from an outsider's perspective. They've wanted to know what the opportunities are for them to work overseas for high tech. I tell them what another HR manager told me in a recent interview:

U.S. companies in our industry are unlikely to recruit somebody from outside to go overseas. They want to send their tried and trusted lieutenants. Being four or five years in one company first of all, and having some high-level performance definitely puts you on that platform. . . . These are jobs for people who have very strong communications and interpersonal skills, very strong influencing skills, good negotiation skills. And are trusted by headquarters management. . . . Having technical skills would be a plus, but a person with technical skills who didn't have the others would fail in the international environment. If you have those [nontechnical] skills, there are a number of roles you can go after; if you have an EE [electrical engineering] degree, there are maybe one or two.

So there is good news and bad news; the good news is that non-technical people actually have a better shot at getting an overseas posting than technical people. The bad news is that you can't just sail into such an assignment; you have to have a track record. Here's an actual case history of how a young woman made this happen for her. She started by getting a lower-level job in an international division of a hardware group:

> I started out as an admin, but after a few months we got a new VP of marketing. He came and asked me what I was doing in that position, and he promoted me to being the program manager of the ISV relationship program. I asked for this because I could see that soon the [availability of] applications were going to be the most important part of the sale. I was to take the ISVs software that ran on our machines and get it localized. That means arranging different levels of support for the software in different countries, and also certain software tools needed to be put into the local language. . . .
>
> I grew my job, broadened it to include how you signed up a vendor. How do you send them a contract, get them on board? Then I started teaching the managers in the field to take that responsibility as a local responsibility, overseas. Then I could take a step back and get more strategic, decide who were the vendors who were bringing us the most business. . . .
>
> I had decided very early on that I wanted to join a company in some kind of international capacity; I wanted the company basically to send me around the world on their books. . . . It was a matter of climbing the ladder and moving up until you became more of a senior manager owning the charter. And from there, in order to understand truly what the business was about, I had to get out of headquarters and move overseas, close to the customers.

She took an assignment in Australia as a business development manager. It took her a little less than five years to go from being an admin to being "a senior manager owning the charter." She had grown her job and won the respect and trust of the vice-president of the international division, and so she got her wish.

The "Area Studies" Delusion

I once worked for a high-tech company that, like every other, really wanted to boost its business in Japan. I happened to meet a young woman who was just out of a prominent midwestern university. She had a bachelor's degree in the particular high-tech field; she had spent six months in Japan in her high school days and had learned Japanese, in which she had a college minor. She wanted desperately to get back to Japan; secondarily, she wanted a job. I passed her resumé and cover letter to a friend who, I thought, would be interested in interviewing her, especially since we were expanding operations in Tokyo, and there would probably be some headcount soon.

To my surprise, my friend did not seem in the least interested. He put the young woman's résumé on a pile of folders on the shelf and, pointing to the stack, uttered the memorable phrase, "They're a dime a dozen."

What? Japanese-speaking, excellent technical education, and a woman to boot (we needed to do better in the EEO department), and she was not even worth an interview? Did anyone counsel this young woman during her college days that even an insider (me) would be unable to get her a lousy fifteen minutes with a hiring manager?

Several years later, looking back at this incident, and with the benefit of having witnessed many similar situations, I can see what went wrong. She was too eager. The great French statesman Talleyrand once advised his ambassadors: "*Surtout, Messieurs, point de zèle,*" which is probably best translated today by the phrase "stay cool." Hiring managers will *never* hire you for an overseas job just because it's what you want most in the whole world and all your education has prepared you for it, as three of your professors have attested in writing. Get into the international division, by all means, and let your boss know that if any Sri Lankans come in for a customer visit, you'd be happy to interpret, given your fluent Singhalese. But none of that *zèle* stuff.

Also, she was too specific. In specifying Japan and emphasizing her experience in that country, she unintentionally sent the message that getting back to Japan was of primary importance, and the job itself came in second.

If you have a good grounding in some international area and you speak a language or two, don't think that that has escaped the attention of the hiring manager (provided, of course, that you included it on your resumé), even if she doesn't allude to it in your discussions. Sometimes hiring managers will bring it up, and may even ask you why you haven't chosen to capitalize on this aspect of your education by heading straight for an international job—perhaps with a bank or the U.S. government.

This isn't a trick question; it merely reflects what the hiring manager thinks she would do, given the same background as the candidate. If this should happen to you during an interview, for heaven's sakes, don't start agreeing with the manager that maybe she's right, and you *should* redirect your job search elsewhere! Keep your eyes on the prize, which is the position you are interviewing for. By all means acknowledge your interest in international opportunities, but state that for the next few years your strong interest is in getting a good grounding in the basics of the business (or in whatever specific opportunity is offered by the position you're discussing).

When You Really Want a Foreign Assignment

It is extremely rare nowadays that anyone is sent over with a full expat package—all the goodies mentioned earlier. In fact, in most of the high-tech industry today, a full package is given only to people who really do *not* necessarily want to work overseas, but who have some special skills and talents that are required for a limited period of time. In order to get these employees to agree to go, the company offers a full plate of inducements. The company has made the calculation that it's worth the high cost to get this person overseas for a year or two.

Where does that leave an ordinary person who really wants to get overseas? Well, how badly do you want to go? If you have a good track record, your boss will support your request, and if you have spotted a need that you can fill, it is possible to make it happen, but the price may well be giving up any thought of getting a full expat package. If you have a house with a mortgage, two kids in school, and a spouse who has a job, you may want to think twice about working overseas without a full package, because you won't be able to afford it. High-tech companies today may offer to send you over as a local employee—that is, they give you a round-trip airline ticket if you're lucky, and a one-way ticket if you're not. Sometimes they will pay for tickets for your family, and sometimes not. Costs of private schools, home leaves, local automobile, and so forth are out, for the most part, though in some cases you might get assistance with locating a place to live, and even some help with the rent (usually this is worked through the local hiring manager at the overseas location). The company will assist you in getting a local work permit, usually valid for two years (and very difficult to get renewed). But only one person in the family benefits from this permit— you. Your spouse may not work, at least not legally. Your children will have to go to local schools, and you'll have to rent or purchase transportation yourself. You'll get no assistance in renting your home in the United States.

This kind of arrangement can put a lot of strain on a relationship. In fact, it can end a relationship. On the other hand, if you are single, relatively young, and ambitious, and you really have the desire to go, it's well worth doing. Having an international stint on your resumé is very desirable in the high-tech industry. The paradox is that this important experience will most likely pay off for you in another company, not the one that sent you overseas. We'll take a look at the reasons for this in a few moments.

Here's how one person worked his deal out for a two-year assignment in Asia. Note that he ended up by negotiating directly with the overseas operation, bypassing his U.S. HR people.

> My package is the most convoluted you'll ever come across. I don't know what label to give myself. The company didn't give me the option to go over as a traditional expat. An expat to me is someone who is paid in U.S. dollars, who goes overseas, and who has money sent to them, and you get a whole lot of other benefits. . . .
>
> When I went overseas, the position I moved into had been open for nine months. They had interviewed locally and couldn't find anybody, so it was very much in the company's interest to send over a head office person who was in charge of that area at home, and to plug them into the country. Because I knew all the contacts at the head office, I knew how to jump-start the program very quickly.
>
> [The U.S. headquarters] did ask me to go, but I also wanted to go. That turned into a big issue, because if the company sends you overseas, you must go as an expat. If you want to go, then they have leeway to kind of pull back elements of the package and say you're going because you asked to. It was a very lousy game they were playing. In the end I went over and decided to be paid as a local in local currency, because the salary was about $40,000 more a year than what the U.S. [HR] people were offering me. I went through my own spreadsheet and realized I was actually better off with the local package. Yes, I had to pay local taxes, but I got a credit against U.S. taxes. I did negotiate assistance with housing, and I had a company car in the end. So I got a couple of perks that were important.

Working in the Overseas Office

The high-tech industry is fast-paced, hard-driving, and values "pushiness"—in the United States. Needless to say, not all foreign cultures take kindly to these characteristics, and when U.S. high-tech managers or individual contributors are assigned overseas, or assign themselves overseas, there can be some rough periods before smooth working relations with nationals of the country of posting are established. Here's the story, told by someone who worked for him, of a very successful manager in the United States, who went overseas to run a sales operation:

> When Tony got over there, he was in typical Tony mode, very aggressive and fast-moving and loud and hard-charging, like most top managers at [company] are. And everybody turned off to him. And within two to three weeks he had absolutely no support from anyone. He realized after a while that you just can't come into a different culture and start pushing things around the way you want them to go.

In that case the new U.S. manager woke up too late; most of his best local nationals—managers and individual contributors—left for other employment in the first three months of his tenure.

Overseas the pace may be different.

Though you may consider yourself to be culturally sensitive, you too may find yourself in a delicate position when it comes to fitting into an overseas operation. A woman who took over a marketing position in Europe told me:

> You have to prove yourself to them—not that they're skeptical, they just want to understand what you're all about. And why did we have to bring someone in from outside the country when there are plenty of capable managers in the country? So they're looking to see you deliver some unique value added that is not available in the local marketplace. . . . For the first four to eight weeks I just walked around on eggshells.

Reentry

The most traumatic part of working overseas in the high-tech industry is your reentry, or attempted reentry, into the U.S. company. Few if any high-tech companies have succeeded in setting up a workable system to facilitate the reentry process, and as a consequence the costly investment in expat employees is often wasted. Both expat and "local hire" employees are often forced to leave their company because there is no job for them when they return. If you accept an overseas assignment, you should be prepared for this. Companies sometimes have the trappings of a system to help returning employees find employment; when the employee first leaves for the assignment, he or she may be assigned a "sponsor," or mentor in headquarters, whose job it is to keep in touch with the employee and assist with relocation into a domestic assignment. This type of system never works. Usually the mentor is in a different job, division, or location by the time the employee is ready to return. In any case, other employees who did not take overseas posts have already targeted the choice positions and have been working to get them for months; the returning employee is a latecomer, having missed out on two or three years of contact and political developments. It is extraordinary that, having selected employees for costly overseas assignments because of their special or even unique talents, the high-tech company does not go to extraordinary lengths to retain them after their assignments are over.

Perhaps this is because U.S. high-tech companies, being generally young, are still quite unsophisticated as regards tackling overseas markets. Most customers in foreign countries like to do business with people they know and trust. In some parts of the world it can take two years to build such a relationship; at that point the American employee is either yanked back home or told that he or she can stay on, but only under local conditions, even when the initial assignment was with an expat package. Many European companies approach their overseas markets quite differently; they have what amounts to a mini-Foreign Service, and employees serve in it for twenty years or more, moving from one post to another, but always within a given region. In Southeast Asia, for example, a British company might post someone in Singapore for three or four years, then move the person to Malaysia for a similar period. This might be followed by a posting to Indonesia, and then Hong Kong, and finally back to Singapore. Such employees become true experts in foreign markets, get to know important government officials on a personal basis, speak the local languages, and generally integrate better into the assignment. European expats, therefore, don't have any problem with repatriation and reintegration into the company, because from the start they are in it for the long haul.

Fortunately for American companies, U.S. technical leadership in the high-tech industry has overcome many shortcomings in sales and marketing. Channels and customers may not be overwhelmingly happy with the service they receive in the area of sales and marketing, but they put up with it to get the products. However, when the technology of the U.S. companies doesn't deliver the goods, foreign competition often wins the day.

The problems faced by returning U.S. expats are illustrated vividly in the following remarks by an individual contributor who had put in two years in Australia for a hardware company:

> [The U.S. company] wasn't interested in me because they were trying to reduce headcount when I returned. I received almost no attention and no assistance as my visa began to wind down. I finally started to make my own arrangements to ship my own stuff back, and the company woke up and realized they were in a poor position and could be sued.
>
> The next thing that happened was they sent me layoff papers before I even got back to the United States. So I cut a deal and said, 'Contractually you are obligated to find me a job, so give me two months to look around and if I don't find anything, then you give me a severance package and I'll leave quite happily.' So that's what happened.

It's amazing how many returning expats speak of having thought of suing or threatening to sue the companies that sent them overseas.

That's because of the breakdown of the reentry process; no one wants to take responsibility, no one has a suitable position for the returning employee, and everyone wishes the problem would go somewhere else.

This sort of problem can even affect those who are very well entrenched in a company. Here's the story of a senior manager who had been with his company almost since its founding, who was very friendly with the president and a number of vice-presidents, who had contributed to the company's success in several key new markets, and who was actively recruited to go overseas for two years:

> It costs the company a fortune to do it [the expat package]. So that's great to get you there and it's great to support you. Now it's time to come home. Your assignment is up. And you say, OK, now what job do I get when I go back? The answer is, go find one.

> It was very scary because I had been following what happened to other expats that went back, and I only knew of one that actually came back to a good job, came back to a job at all. So I came back in December [on a brief trip] and I sent an E-mail to all the top people in the company and basically started trolling for jobs. The response was, "great, come in, love to talk to you, let's see what might be available."

This manager was lucky, because a good job did open up while he was in the United States, and thanks to his connections at the top of the company, he was able to get it. But as he observed:

> If that spot hadn't been there, I would have come back from that trip with nothing. And I was facing my visa expiring in sixty days.

> I think it's a case of the company's not having the maturity as an organization to capture and leverage the investment that's been made in the people. People sent overseas on postings are not the bottom 10 percent of the company, they're the top 10 percent. And if we're making this kind of investment, it's an absolute sin that we're not recapturing this investment.

> But what happens is the people come back at different points in time and they try to reenter the organization, and there's nothing there that can take advantage of the value that the person has built up.

A business development manager working in Buenos Aires was three months from returning to the United States after a two-year posting. He was visited by the vice-president for Latin America, who told him that because business in Japan was down, all salary and administration budgets in the international division were going to be cut for the third time, and that there would be no job for him when he returned. He was given three months' salary starting from the time his posting ended. He therefore spent most of the rest of his assignment trying to find another position with another company in the United States. This was difficult to do, because he could not take time off to return on a job-hunting trip. In the end he did find a job, but the company that had sent him overseas had certainly lost his full attention to his job for a period of several months.

Final Words on Overseas High-Tech Assignments

In some ways, working in an overseas high-tech assignment is like working in a startup: You generally have much more authority and responsibility than you did back in the States, and you're part of a smaller group that can develop a lot of cohesion. Working in a foreign environment, if you have even a modicum of sensitivity, can make you more aware of how others see your home country, and it can make you more aware and respectful of another culture. The high-tech industry needs foreign markets, and should you decide to continue in an international career, your overseas experience will make you very much more attractive as a potential hire to other companies, provided you work it so that you approach them when you're still working for your present company.

And if you decide to return to the United States for good, your life will be richer in ways you can appreciate only when you have been through the overseas experience.

Leaving an overseas posting can be a wrenching time, and can leave you with a sense of loss once you return. Is it worth it? You bet it is! If you can make it happen, do it!

9
Final Words of Wisdom

This book began with a quotation from Carlyle about finding your work—that is, an occupation for which you are so suited that in it you find "blessedness." The search for such work has to start with an understanding of the kind of person you are, as was mentioned in Chapter 3. That's often not so easy. François Villon, the rogue poet of Paris, said, "I know everything, except myself." That was over five centuries ago. And 1,500 years before that, a Roman named Plautus observed, "No man is wise enough by himself."

One of the purposes of this book is to give you a feeling for what life in the high-tech industry would be like. If you have come this far and are still not sure how well you would fit in, now is the time to get better acquainted with yourself. Visit career centers and talk to professionals who can help you learn more about the kind of person you are. You may be fortunate enough to find someone who has herself had some years' experience in the industry, but that's not essential. Remember that there are tests to help determine how well you'll fit into certain environments. You know the environment from reading the book, so you can make the call on moving to high tech after getting your test results.

The high-tech industry can offer you a lifetime of learning and personal growth. And it can pay the rent plus utilities, with enough left over for a vacation in Hawaii. Few people have left it and found much contentment in other pursuits; it's just too exciting and satisfying.

Try it and see for yourself!

Index